TEIKYO WESTMAR UNIV

W9-BOA-247

ECONOMIC SANCTIONS IN SUPPORT OF FOREIGN POLICY GOALS

Gary Clyde Hufbauer and Jeffrey J. Schott
assisted by
Kimberly Ann Elliott

92-1372

INSTITUTE FOR INTERNATIONAL ECONOMICS
WASHINGTON, DC
OCTOBER 1983

Gary Clyde Hufbauer is a Senior Fellow at the Institute for International Economics. He was formerly Deputy Director of the International Law Institute at Georgetown University, Deputy Assistant Secretary for International Trade and Investment Policy of the US Treasury, Director of the International Tax Staff at the Treasury, and Professor of Economics at the University of New Mexico. Dr. Hufbauer has published numerous studies on international trade, investment, and tax issues.

Jeffrey J. Schott is a Visiting Fellow at the Institute for International Economics and is associated with the Diebold Institute for Public Policy Studies in New York. He was formerly a senior associate at the Carnegie Endowment for International Peace, during which time he carried out his initial work on this study; an international economist in the US Treasury Department, and a member of the research staff at the Brookings Institution.

Kimberly Ann Elliott is a Research Assistant at the Institute for International Economics. A 1982 graduate of Austin College with honors in political science, she is currently pursuing a Master's degree in international relations at the Johns Hopkins School of Advanced International Studies.

INSTITUTE FOR INTERNATIONAL ECONOMICS
C. Fred Bergsten, *Director*
Kathleen A. Lynch, *Director of Publications*

The Institute for International Economics was created, and is principally funded, by the German Marshall Fund of the United States.

The views expressed in this publication are those of the authors. The publication is part of the research program of the Institute, as endorsed by its Board of Directors, but does not necessarily reflect the views of individual members of the Board of the Advisory Committee.

Copyright © 1983 Institute for International Economics. All rights reserved. No part of this book may be reproduced or utilized in any form or by any means, electronic or mechanical, including photocopying, recording, or by information storage or retrieval system, without written permission from the Institute.

First Printing October 1983
Second Printing June 1986

Library of Congress Cataloging-in-Publication Data

Hufbauer, Gary Clyde.
    Economic sanctions in support of foreign policy goals.

    (Policy analyses in international economics; 6)
    Bibliography: p.
    1. International economic relations. 2. Sanctions (International law). I. Schott, Jeffrey J., 1949–   . II. Elliott, Kimberly Ann, 1960–   . III. Title. IV. Series.
HF1412.H83 1983   382'.3   83-12829
ISBN 0-88132-014-5

Contents

TEXT TABLES

INSTITUTE FOR INTERNATIONAL ECONOMICS
11 Dupont Circle, NW, Washington, DC 20036
(202) 328–0583 Telex: 248329 CEIP

C. Fred Bergsten, *Director*

BOARD OF DIRECTORS

Peter G. Peterson, *Chairman*
Raymond Barre
W. Michael Blumenthal
Douglas A. Fraser
Alan Greenspan
Abdlatif Y. al-Hamad
Reginald H. Jones
Frank E. Loy
Donald F. McHenry
Saburo Okita
I.G. Patel
Karl Otto Pöhl
Donna E. Shalala
Mario Henrique Simonsen
Anthony M. Solomon
John N. Turner
Dennis Weatherstone
Andrew Young

Ex officio
C. Fred Bergsten
Richard N. Cooper

ADVISORY COMMITTEE

Richard N. Cooper, *Chairman*
Robert Baldwin
Lester Brown
Rimmer de Vries
Carlos Diaz-Alejandro
Rudiger Dornbusch
Robert J. Flanagan
Isaiah Frank
Herbert Giersch
Gottfried Haberler
Mahbub ul Haq
Arnold C. Harberger
Dale E. Hathaway
Peter B. Kenen
Lawrence R. Klein
Ryutaro Komiya
Lawrence B. Krause
Assar Lindbeck
Harald B. Malmgren
Richard R. Nelson
Joseph S. Nye, Jr.
Rudolph A. Oswald
Ernest Stern
Philip K. Verleger
Henry Wallich
Marina Whitman
Alan Wm. Wolff

Preface

This publication attempts to present a comprehensive analysis of the sanctions issue. In an effort to achieve the Institute's objective of making its work available to a wide audience, the study summarizes quite briefly, in footnotes and annexes, much of the technical analysis underlying its findings and conclusions. For those interested in the detailed case studies, the complete methodology used, and more elaborate presentation of the underlying data, the Institute will shortly publish a volume entitled *Economic Sanctions Reconsidered: History and Current Policy*, also by Gary Clyde Hufbauer and Jeffrey J. Schott. This technique of publishing a shorter policy oriented version and a longer, more detailed version of the same study follows the approach previously developed in our work on *International Debt, IMF Conditionality*, and *Trade Policy in the 1980s*.

The Institute for International Economics is a private nonprofit research institution for the study and discussion of international economic policy. Its purpose is to analyze important issues in that area, and to develop and communicate practical new approaches for dealing with them.

The Institute was created in November 1981 through a generous commitment of funds from the German Marshall Fund of the United States. Financial support has been received from other private foundations and corporations. The Institute is completely nonpartisan. It wishes to thank the Carnegie Endowment for International Peace for its assistance in carrying out this project.

The Board of Directors bears overall responsibility for the Institute and gives general guidance and approval to its research program—including identification of topics that are likely to become important to international economic policymakers over the medium run (generally, one to three years) and which thus should be addressed by the Institute. The Director of the Institute, working closely with the staff and outside Advisory Committee, is responsible for the development of particular projects and makes the final decision to publish an individual study.

The Institute hopes that its studies and other activities will contribute to building a stronger foundation for international economic policy around the world. Comments as to how it can best do so are invited from readers of these publications.

C. FRED BERGSTEN
Director

1 Introduction

The US grain embargo against the Soviet Union and US restrictions on the Soviet-European gas pipeline rekindled a heated international debate over the use of economic sanctions in pursuit of foreign policy goals. Advocates regard such measures as an important weapon in the arsenal of economic warfare. Skeptical observers question whether sanctions are an effective instrument of foreign policy and whether the costs of sanctions are worth the benefits derived.

To put these issues in perspective, we have delved into the rich history of the use of sanctions by a number of countries in the twentieth century in order to identify circumstances in which economic sanctions can "succeed" in attaining foreign policy goals. We believe it is useful to look beyond actions taken in the context of East-West relations; while the Soviet cases are important, they do not tell the whole story. Indeed, sanctions have been imposed in the East-West context in only about 10 percent of the cases we have studied.

Our study concentrates on three central questions: What factors in a sanctions episode—both political and economic—usually result in the achievement of foreign policy goals? What are the costs of sanctions to both target and sender[1] countries, and to what extent do they influence policy decisions? What lessons can be drawn from this experience to guide the policymaker on the use of sanctions in the future?

Lessons Drawn from Case Studies

Much has been written about the use of economic sanctions in the conduct of foreign policy, and most of the literature takes the form of case studies. In this study we attempt to extract propositions of general validity from that literature.

The starting point for our analysis is the list shown in table 1.1 (at the end of this chapter) of 99 cases of economic sanctions, beginning with the economic blockade of Germany in World War I. At this writing, we have abstracted some 78 cases, those marked by an asterisk in table 1.1. The

---

1. We use the term "sender" to denote the country whose foreign policy goals are being pursued at least in part through the threat or imposition of economic sanctions. A synonymous term often found in the literature is "sanctioner."

abstracts summarize the key events, goals, responses, economic costs, and assessments of each case. (Because each abstract cites sources, we have minimized source notes in this monograph. A bibliography of general references follows chapter 5.) Unless otherwise indicated, the propositions and generalizations in this monograph are based on the 78 cases for which abstracts have been prepared, not the entire list of 99 cases. The 21 cases not yet abstracted are mostly smaller episodes, entailing relatively modest objectives. Thus, the coverage of this monograph is somewhat biased towards the "big case."

A sample abstract, the case of the *League of Nations v. Italy* (1935–36: Ethiopia), appears as appendix A. Abstracts will eventually be prepared for all 99 cases and published in our forthcoming volume, *Economic Sanctions Reconsidered: History and Current Policy*. Because these abstracts summarize each episode, and because detailed narratives can be found in the literature, we deliberately refrain from extensive descriptions of the events of individual episodes in this monograph.

The cases listed in table 1.1 plainly do not include all instances since World War I of economic leverage applied by one sovereign state to try to change the conduct of another. Boundaries must be drawn to distinguish economic sanctions from other economic instruments and to separate foreign policy goals from other goals at home and abroad. Our boundaries may be described in the following way.

We define economic sanctions to mean the deliberate government-inspired withdrawal, or threat of withdrawal, of "customary" trade or financial relations. "Customary" does not mean "contractual"; it simply means levels that would probably have occurred in the absence of sanctions. Generally we exclude instances where economic incentives are used to achieve foreign policy goals. However, when incentives are closely connected with economic sanctions ("carrot-and-stick" diplomacy), they are covered in our abstracts and analysis.

We define foreign policy goals to encompass changes actually and purportedly sought by the sender state—the country imposing sanctions—in the political behavior of the target state. We rely on public statements of senior officials of the sender country, supplemented by the assessment of historians of each particular episode, for a definition of the foreign policy goals sought through the use of sanctions.

We exclude from foreign policy goals the normal realm of objectives sought in banking, commercial, and tax negotiations between sovereign states. However, many of our cases deal with attempts to settle expropriation disputes using economic leverage. Many expropriation episodes harbor political disputes that go beyond compensation issues, and those are the episodes we seek to cover.

Sanctions also serve important domestic political purposes in addition to whatever change they may bring about in the behavior of foreign states. As David Lloyd George remarked in the celebrated League of Nations foray in 1935 against Italy, "[Sanctions] came too late to save Abyssinia, but they are just in the nick of time to save the [British] Government."[2]

The same is true today. What president—or Kremlin leader for that matter—has not been obsessed with the need to demonstrate leadership, to take initiatives to shape world affairs, or at least to react forcefully to adverse developments? And what president—or Kremlin leader—wants to go to war to make his point? The desire to be seen acting forcefully, but not to precipitate bloodshed, can easily overshadow specific foreign policy goals. Indeed, one suspects that in some cases domestic political goals were the motivating force behind the imposition of sanctions. Such measures often serve to distract attention from domestic ills and to galvanize public support for the government, either by inflaming patriotic fever (illustrated by US sanctions against Japan prior to World War II) or by quenching the public thirst for action (illustrated by US sanctions against Qadhafi's adventurism in northern Africa). However, we have left to others the arduous task of unearthing the domestic side of the story and determining whether sanctions in fact satisfy domestic political purposes.

In this study we make no attempt to evaluate the merits of foreign policy goals pursued through the use of sanctions. We have opinions on those goals, but we doubt that many readers are eager to discover the collective wisdom of Hufbauer, Schott, and Elliott on the morality, for example, of destabilizing the Trujillo government in 1960–61. Similarly, we do not explore the fascinating international law questions raised by the imposition of sanctions, in particular the definition and proper limitation of "extraterritorial" measures. Much literature is devoted to these questions and we could not, in a short monograph, usefully contribute to the legal debate (see, for example, Marcuss and Richard, 1981; Rosenthal and Knighton, 1982; Moyer and Mabry, 1983).

Table 1.1 probably omits many uses of sanctions imposed between powers of the second and third rank. These cases are often not well-documented in the English language, and we did not have adequate resources to study source

---

2. Peter Rowland, *David Lloyd George: A Biography* (New York: Macmillan, 1975), p. 723.

material in foreign languages. We have also no doubt overlooked instances where sanctions were imposed by major powers in comparative secrecy to achieve relatively modest goals. To the extent of these omissions, our generalizations will not adequately reflect the experience of the twentieth century.

Historical Overview

Economic sanctions entered the diplomatic armory long before World War I. Indeed the technique was used in ancient Greece. The most celebrated occasion was Pericles' Megarian decree, enacted in 432 BC, in response to Megarian expansion and the kidnap of three Aspasian females. Thucydides accords the decree only minor notice; by contrast, Aristophanes in the *Archarnians* (lines 530–43), assigns the Megarian decree a major role in triggering the Peloponnesian War[3]:

Then Pericles the Olympian in his wrath / thundered lightened, threw Hellas into confusion,/ passed laws that were written like drinking songs / [decreeing] the Megarians shall not be on our land, in our market,/ on the sea or on the continent./ /Then the Megarians, since they were starving little by little, begged the Lacedae-monians to have the decree /arising from the three strumpets withdrawn./ But we were unwilling, though they asked us many times. Then came the clash of the shields./ Someone will say it was not right. But say, then, what was. /Come, if a Lacedaemonian sailed out in a boat /and denounced and confiscated a Seriphian puppy, /would you have sat still?

Despite the rich history of episodes from ancient Greece through the nineteenth century, we start with World War I both because earlier episodes are less well documented and because lessons from the distant past may seem less relevant to today's problems. However, by way of historical perspective, table 1.2 (at the end of this chapter) lists selected pre-World War I instances of economic sanctions. Most of these episodes foreshadowed or accompanied warfare. Only after World War I was extensive attention given to the notion that economic sanctions might substitute for armed hostilities.

Through World War II, the objectives sought with the use of sanctions

---

3. See Charles Fornara, ''Plutarch and the Megarian decree,'' 24 *Yale Classical Studies,* (1975).

retained a distinctive martial flavor. Sanctions were usually imposed to disrupt military adventures or to complement a broader war effort. Of the 11 cases we have identified in table 1.1 between 1914 and 1940, all but 2 are linked to military action. Four of the cases involved League of Nations attempts, through collective action, to settle disputes. These efforts had varied results: from the successful threat of economic sanctions that led Greece to back down from its incursion into Bulgaria in 1925 to the League's celebrated failure at persuading Italy to withdraw from Ethiopia in the mid-1930s.

In the period following World War II, other foreign policy motives became increasingly common, but sanctions were still deployed to force a target country to withdraw its troops from border skirmishes, to abandon plans of territorial acquisition, or to desist from other military adventures. In most instances in the postwar period where economic pressure was brought to bear against the exercise of military power, the United States played the role of international policeman. For example, the United States was able to coerce the Netherlands into backing away from its military efforts in 1948–49 to forestall the Indonesian federation; in 1956, the United States pressed the French and British into leaving the Suez; and in the early 1960s, the United States persuaded Egypt to withdraw its troops from Yemen and the Congo by withholding development and PL-480 food aid.

More recent attempts have not been as successful. Turkish troops continue to be stationed in Cyprus almost a decade after the invasion and in spite of US economic pressure in the mid-1970s. The grain and Olympic boycott of the USSR did not discourage the Soviet occupation of Afghanistan. Indeed, major powers have never been able to deter the military adventures of other major powers simply through the use of economic sanctions.

Closely related to military adventure cases are the episodes where sanctions are imposed to impair the economic capability of the target country, thereby limiting its potential for military activity. This was one rationale for the broad-based multilateral controls on strategic trade that the United States instituted against the USSR and China in the late 1940s, and was cited by US officials in defense of recent sanctions against the USSR following the invasion of Afghanistan and the crisis in Poland. It is doubtful whether these cases have yielded positive results, not least because it is difficult to link the military capabilities of a major power with marginal degrees of economic deprivation.

In this monograph we do not evaluate the narrowly defined national security issues that arise in cases where sanctions are deployed to deprive the USSR and other countries from access to goods and technology with a direct military application. While attempts to impair the military potential of an adversary usually involve these narrowly defined national security questions—what military hardware can be denied the adversary?—in these cases the sender country also seeks to limit the foreign policy options of the target state. Thus, in our view, the COCOM and CHINCOM controls[4] were aimed both at restricting strategic exports to the USSR and China to prevent technological advances in weaponry, and at impairing the ability of the Soviet and Chinese economies to support an expanded military machine. The latter goal—to inhibit potential Soviet and Chinese foreign policy responses by limiting their national capability to support a military machine—is the reason why these cases are included in our analysis.

Sanctions have also been deployed in pursuit of a number of other foreign policy goals. Especially noteworthy is the frequent resort to sanctions to help destabilize foreign governments, usually in the context of a foreign policy dispute involving other issues. Destabilization episodes have often found a superpower pitted against a smaller country. The United States has engaged in destabilization efforts 12 times, often against neighboring countries in the hemisphere such as Cuba, the Dominican Republic, Nicaragua, Brazil, and Chile. Sanctions contributed at least in part to the overthrow of Trujillo in 1961, Goulart in 1964, and Allende in 1973; on the other hand, Castro's Cuba and the Sandinistas in Nicaragua have not succumbed to US pressure, in large measure due to compensating aid from the USSR.

The USSR has also picked on its neighbors, though somewhat less successfully. Almost every time the USSR used sanctions in an effort to topple a government of the socialist bloc, it failed (Yugoslavia in 1948, China in 1960, Albania in 1961, and Romania in 1965); the only success story came when the USSR coerced Finland into adopting a more pliant attitude toward Soviet policies during the "Nightfrost Crisis" of 1958. Finally, the United Kingdom also has participated in the destabilization game through the use of economic sanctions to topple hostile or repressive regimes

---

4. *United States and COCOM v. USSR and COMECON* (1948–), and *United States and CHINCOM v. China* (1949–70). COCOM, the Coordinating Committee for Multilateral Export Controls, and CHINCOM, the China Committee, are informal groups of NATO countries (plus Japan) which attempt to limit the shipment of strategic goods (broadly and narrowly defined) to the Soviet Union and China, respectively. COMECON, the Council for Mutual Economic Assistance, is an organization established in 1949 to facilitate economic cooperation between the USSR and its satellites.

in areas where Britain once exercised colonial influence—Iran in 1951–53, Rhodesia in 1965–79, and Uganda in 1972–79.

Since the early 1960s, sanctions have been deployed in support of numerous other foreign policy goals, most of them relatively modest compared to the pursuit of war, peace, and political destabilization. For example, sanctions have been used on behalf of efforts to protect human rights, to halt nuclear proliferation, to settle expropriation claims, and to combat international terrorism. Here again, the United States has played the dominant role as guardian of its version of global morality.

Following a series of congressionally inspired initiatives beginning in 1973, human rights became a "cause célèbre" of the Carter administration. In the early phase, country-specific riders were attached to military aid bills requiring the Nixon and Ford administrations to deny or reduce assistance to countries found abusing human rights. In the later phase, President Carter adopted the congressional mandate as his own guiding light. Eventually, many countries in Latin America and elsewhere became targets of US sanctions.

Sanctions were also frequently used, by both the United States and Canada, to enforce compliance with nuclear nonproliferation safeguards. In 1974, Canada acted to deter Pakistan from proceeding with underground nuclear test explosions, and tried to control the reprocessing of spent fuel in both India and Pakistan to guard against weapons production. The United States joined the Canadians in applying financial pressure on South Korea to forestall its purchase of a nuclear reprocessing plant. Subsequently, the United States imposed sanctions on shipments of nuclear fuel and technology to South Africa, Taiwan, Brazil, Argentina, India, and Pakistan in similar attempts to secure adequate multilateral surveillance of nuclear facilities.

Since World War II, the United States has used sanctions eight times in its efforts to negotiate compensation for property expropriated by foreign governments. In almost all the cases, the United States hoped to go beyond the claims issue and resolve conflicting political philosophies. This was true the first time the US pressured Iran—seeking the overthrow of the Mussadiq regime—and was behind US efforts to undermine Castro in Cuba, Goulart in Brazil, and Allende in Chile.

Antiterrorism has been another of the modest (but important) policy goals sought by the United States through the imposition of economic sanctions. A wave of international plane hijackings in the 1960s and 1970s, and the massacre of Israeli athletes at the Munich Olympics in 1972, focused world attention on terrorism. The hijacking problem was greatly reduced through international hijacking agreements—including one signed in 1973 by the

United States and Cuba. Lethal terrorist raids, often funded by radical, oil-rich countries, have proven much harder to control. In 1980, following a congressional directive, the US State Department branded four countries—Libya, Syria, Iraq, and South Yemen—as international outlaws because of their support of terrorist activities. The United States soon imposed sanctions on Libya and Iraq in an attempt to limit their ability as suppliers of military equipment to terrorist groups.

This brief historical review illustrates the important role that economic sanctions have played since World War I in the conduct of US foreign policy. Of the 99 cases documented in table 1.1, the United States, either alone or in concert with its allies, has deployed sanctions 62 times. Other significant users have been the United Kingdom (18 instances, often in cooperation with the League of Nations and the United Nations); the Soviet Union (10 uses, usually against recalcitrant satellites); and the Arab League and its members (6 uses of its new-found oil muscle).

This overview also demonstrates that sanctions have been deployed more frequently with each passing decade. Table 1.3 summarizes the record: first, the number of sanctions episodes initiated in each five-year period beginning with 1911–15; second, the total cost imposed on target countries every fifth year beginning with 1915 (expressed as an annualized figure in current US dollars); and third, for comparison, the value of world exports (expressed in current US dollars). The summary in table 1.3 indicates that the quinquennial level of new episodes has increased from under 5 in the pre-1945 period to approximately 10 to 15 in the post-1960 period. The annual cost imposed on target countries was quite high in 1915, on account of World War I; it fell markedly thereafter, and has since risen from very low levels in the 1920s and 1930s to some $1.5 billion and higher in the post-1965 period. The aggregate cost of sanctions peaked in 1980, with almost $5 billion of costs imposed on target countries.

While sanctions activity has grown, particularly in recent decades, it has not kept pace over the long haul with the very buoyant growth of world trade. The level of world trade (expressed in current dollars) expanded more than a hundred times between 1915 and 1980. Compared to total world trade flows, the cost imposed on target countries is barely a ripple.

The Cyclical Popularity of Sanctions

Like other fashions, economic sanctions wax and wane in popularity. After World War I, great hopes were held out for the "economic weapon," with

President Woodrow Wilson the leading advocate. Speaking in Indianapolis in 1919 he said:[5]

A nation that is boycotted is a nation that is in sight of surrender. Apply this economic, peaceful, silent, deadly remedy and there will be no need for force. It is a terrible remedy. It does not cost a life outside the nation boycotted, but it brings a pressure upon the nation which, in my judgment, no modern nation could resist.

The League of Nations enjoyed minor success with the use of sanctions against smaller powers in the 1920s and 1930s. But with the failure of the League's campaign against Italy, the reputation of the "economic weapon" correspondingly sank. Scholars were quick to point out that sanctions had not in fact been used decisively against Italy, but the public at large simply concluded that sanctions were not equal to the task.

The reputation of the "economic weapon" was somewhat rehabilitated by the contribution of the naval blockade of Europe and the preemptive buying of strategic materials by the Allies to the ultimate defeat of Germany and Japan during World War II. Sanctions were used frequently and with some success in the late 1940s and 1950s, but they did not again attract public notice until the US campaign against Cuba and the UK/UN campaign against Rhodesia in the 1960s. Overoptimistic British pronouncements in the Rhodesian case and the considerable success of Cuba—with massive aid from the Soviet Union—in withstanding economic pressure again fostered disillusion. Disillusion grew progressively more fashionable with the extensive American reliance on sanctions, and a series of conspicuous failures, in the 1970s and early 1980s.

Have we reached the bottom of the current wave of disfavor over the use of sanctions? We have no crystal ball, but we would suggest that the "economic weapon" will not regain a measure of respectability in the years ahead unless sanctions are deployed more judiciously.

Whatever the cycle of fashion, our purpose in this study is to distinguish between circumstances in which economic sanctions make some contribution to the pursuit of foreign policy goals, and circumstances in which sanctions achieve very little.

---

5. See Saul K. Padover, ed., *Wilson's Ideals* (Washington: American Council on Public Affairs, 1942), p. 108.

Sender Countries and Their Motives

Sanctions are part and parcel of international diplomacy, a tool to coerce target governments into particular avenues of response. The use of sanctions presupposes the sender country's desire to "interfere in the internal affairs" of the target government.

Among the cases we have documented, the countries that impose sanctions generally are large nations that pursue an active foreign policy. To be sure, there are instances of neighborhood fights (*Indonesia v. Malaysia*, 1963–66; *Spain v. United Kingdom*, 1954–   ). But in the main, sanctions have been used by big powers—precisely because they are big and can seek to influence events on a global scale. Instances of the collective use of sanctions—the League of Nations against Italy in 1935–36, the United Nations against Rhodesia in 1965–79, the Western Allies against Germany and Japan, 1939–45—are in fact usually episodes of major powers enlisting their smaller allies.

"Demonstration of resolve" has often supplied the driving force behind the imposition of sanctions. This is particularly true for the United States, which frequently has deployed sanctions to try to assert its leadership in world affairs. US presidents seemingly feel compelled to dramatize their opposition to foreign misdeeds, even when the likelihood of changing behavior in the target country seems remote. In these cases sanctions often are imposed because the cost of inaction—in lost confidence at home and abroad in the ability or willingness of the US to act—is seen as greater than the cost of the sanctions. Indeed, such action is often expected by the international community—to demonstrate moral outrage and to reassure its allies that the United States will stand by its international commitments. The impact of such moral and psychological factors on the decision to impose sanctions should not be underestimated, even if it is hard to document.

"Deterrence" is another frequently cited reason for sanctions: supposedly a sender country can discourage future objectionable policies by increasing the associated costs. Two recent cases (*United States v. USSR* over Afghanistan from 1980 forward and the *United States v. Libya* over terrorism from 1978 forward) suggest that it is difficult, if not impossible, to determine whether sanctions are an effective deterrent.

Finally, sanctions are used as a surrogate for other measures. A diplomatic slap on the wrist may not hit where it hurts. More extreme measures, such as covert action or military measures, may be excessive. Sanctions provide a popular middle road: they add "teeth" to international diplomacy—even if the bark is worse than the bite.

In a sense, the imposition of sanctions conveys a triple signal: to the target country it says the sender does not condone your actions; to allies, it says that words will be supported with deeds; to domestic audiences it says the sender's government will act to safeguard the nation's vital interests.

The parallels between the motives for sanctions and the three basic purposes of criminal law are unmistakable: to punish, to deter, and to rehabilitate. Countries that impose sanctions, like states that incarcerate criminals, may find their hopes of rehabilitation unrealized, but they may be quite satisfied with whatever punishment and deterrence are accomplished. Nevertheless, in judging the success of sanctions, we confine our examination to changes in the policies and capabilities of the target country.

Limitations on the Use of Sanctions

Not all sanctions succeed in terms of changing the behavior of foreign countries. One reason for failure is plain: the sanctions imposed may simply be inadequate to achieve the objectives sought—the goals may be too elusive, the means too gentle, or cooperation from other countries, when needed, too tepid.

A second reason for failure is that sanctions may create their own antidotes. In particular, economic sanctions may unify the target country both in support of the government and in search of commercial alternatives. This outcome was evident in a number of episodes; for example, a nationalistic reaction seems to have plagued the League of Nations actions against Italy in 1935–36, USSR sanctions against Yugoslavia in 1948–55, US measures against Indonesia in 1963–66, and UN actions against Rhodesia in 1965–79. As Mussolini put the matter in 1935: "To sanctions of an economic character we will reply with our discipline, with our sobriety, and with our spirit of sacrifice."[6]

A third reason for the unsuccessful application of economic pressure is that sanctions may prompt powerful allies of the target country to lend support, largely offsetting whatever deprivation results from the sanctions themselves. In the period since World War II, offsetting compensation has occurred most conspicuously in episodes where the big powers were caught

---

6. Robin Renwick, *Economic Sanctions,* Harvard Studies in International Affairs No. 45 (Cambridge, Mass.: Harvard University Center for International Affairs, 1981), p. 18.

up in ideological conflict over the policies of a smaller nation: *USSR v. Yugoslavia* (1948–55), *United States v. Cuba* (1960–   ), *USSR v. Albania* (1961–82), and *United States v. Nicaragua* (1981–   ). Another example, with different historical origins, is the Arab League campaign against Israel, a campaign that has helped ensure a continuing flow of public and private assistance to Israel from the United States and Western Europe.

A fourth reason for failure is that economic sanctions create their own backlash, abroad and at home. Allies abroad may simply not share the goals of the sender country. As a result, they may, in the first instance, ask exasperating questions about the probability of a successful outcome; in the second instance, they may refuse to take stern measures against the target country, thereby making the sender's own initiatives seem all the more futile; finally, they may revolt and enforce national antisanctions laws, such as the US antiboycott provisions and the British Protection of Trading Interests Act, to counteract the impact of sanctions on their own foreign policy and economic interests. The protective legal barrier is a relatively new development, but one that has spread to a number of countries— France, Denmark, Australia, and others—whose firms have been victimized by the often errant aim of a sender state imposing sanctions.

The backlash from the sender's allies may be exacerbated if attempts are made to enforce the sanctions on an extraterritorial basis, as was done in the recent pipeline case. The Europeans refused to cooperate with the United States; indeed, they wondered who the "real" target of the sanctions was: the target *country* subject to sanctions, or their own *firms,* whose trade was being hit by the measures. The internecine feud that ensued between the United States and Europe undercut the economic and psychological force of the sanctions, rendering the action ineffective.

Business firms at home may experience severe losses when sanctions interrupt trade and financial contacts. Moreover, they may lose their reputation for reliability. Outcries from US business against both the grain embargo and the pipeline sanctions arose as much from the fear of future competitive weakness as "unreliable suppliers" as from the immediate sacrifice of grain, pipelayer, and gas turbine sales to the Soviet Union. After the first flush of patriotic enthusiasm, such complaints can undermine a sanctions initiative.

These assorted pitfalls are well-known to most policy officials, and they can hardly escape the briefing memoranda prepared for world leaders. Why then are sanctions so frequently used? In the first place, sanctions have not been, on balance, nearly so unsuccessful as recent episodes directed against the USSR would suggest. Chapters 3, 4, and 5 attempt to provide a rounded view of success and failure, measured in foreign policy terms. In the second place, world leaders often find the most obvious alternatives to economic sanctions—military action or diplomatic protest—too massive or too meager. Sanctions can provide a satisfying theatrical display, yet avoid the high costs of war.

Plan of the Monograph

In chapter 2, we examine the components of a sanctions episode. In a simple and crude way, we attempt to quantify a number of dimensions. We explain our definition of "success," our scheme for distinguishing objectives, our scale of international cooperation, and our measurement of economic costs. In chapter 3, we assess sanctions episodes in terms of their political variables. In chapter 4, we summarize the economic variables in a sanctions episode, and relate economic costs to the measure of success achieved. In chapter 5, we derive general lessons from the cases studied and suggest a list of nine commandments that sender countries might follow to improve their prospects for achieving foreign policy goals.

TABLE 1.1   **Chronological summary of economic sanctions for foreign policy goals, 1914–83**

Case number	Principal sender	Target country	Active years	Goals of sender country
14-1*	United Kingdom	Germany	1914–18	Military victory
17-1*	United States	Japan	1917	Use shipping to help Allies in World War I
18-1*	United Kingdom	USSR	1918–20	(1) Renew support for Allies in World War I (2) Destabilize Bolshevik regime
21-1*	United Kingdom and League of Nations	Yugoslavia	1921	Block Yugoslav attempts to wrest territory from Albania; retain 1913 borders.
25-1*	League of Nations	Greece	1925	Withdraw from occupation of Bulgarian territory
32-1*	League of Nations	Paraguay, Bolivia	1932–35	Settle the Chaco War
33-1*	United Kingdom	USSR	1933	Release two British citizens
35-1*	League of Nations	Italy	1935–36	Withdraw Italian troops from Ethiopia
38-1*	United Kingdom and United States	Mexico	1938–47	Settle expropriation claims
39-1*	Alliance Powers	Germany, later Japan	1939–45	Military victory
40-1*	United States	Japan	1940–41	Withdraw from Southeast Asia
44-1*	United States	Argentina	1944–47	(1) Remove Nazi influence (2) Destabilize Peron government
46-1*	Arab League	Israel	1946–	Create a homeland for Palestinians

TABLE 1.1   **Chronological summary of economic sanctions for foreign policy goals, 1914–83** (*continued*)

Case number	Principal sender	Target country	Active years	Goals of sender country
48-1*	United States	Netherlands	1948–49	Recognize Republic of Indonesia
48-2	India	Hyderabad	1948	Assimilate Hyderabad into India
48-3*	USSR	United States, United Kingdom, and France	1948–49	(1) Prevent formation of a West German government (2) Assimilate West Berlin into East Germany
48-4*	USSR	Yugoslavia	1948–55	(1) Rejoin Soviet camp (2) Destabilize Tito government
48-5*	United States and COCOM	USSR and COMECON	1948–	(1) Deny strategic materials (2) Impair Soviet military potential
49-1	West Germany	USSR	1949–69	Concessions on reunification
49-2*	United States and CHINCOM	China	1949–70	(1) Retaliation for Communist takeover and subsequent assistance to North Korea (2) Deny strategic and other materials
50-1	United States	North Korea	1950–53	Withdraw attack on South Korea
51-1*	United Kingdom and United States	Iran	1951–53	(1) Reverse the nationalization of oil facilities (2) Destabilize Mussadiq government
54-1*	USSR	Australia	1954	Repatriate a Soviet defector
54-2	India	Goa	1954–61	Assimilate Goa into India

(*continued overleaf*)

TABLE 1.1   Chronological summary of economic sanctions for foreign policy goals, 1914–83 (*continued*)

Case number	Principal sender	Target country	Active years	Goals of sender country
54-3*	Spain	United Kingdom	1954–	Gain sovereignty over Gibraltar
56-1*	United States	Israel	1956–	(1) Withdraw from Sinai (2) Implement UN Resolution 242; (3) Push Palestinian autonomy talks
56-2	United Arab Republic	United States and Europe	1956	Prompt Israel, UK, and France to withdraw from Sinai and Suez Canal
56-3*	United States	United Kingdom and France	1956	Withdraw from Suez
56-4*	United States	Laos	1956–62	(1) Destabilize Prince Souvanna Phouma government (2) Destabilize General Phoumi government (3) Prevent Communist takeover
57-1*	Indonesia	Netherlands	1957–62	Control of West Irian
58-1*	USSR	Finland	1958–59	Adopt pro-USSR policies
58-2	United States	North Vietnam, later Vietnam	1958–	(1) Impede military effectiveness of North Vietnam (2) Retribution for aggression in South Vietnam
60-1*	United States	Dominican Republic	1960–62	(1) Cease subversion in Venezuela (2) Destabilize Trujillo government
60-2*	USSR	China	1960–70	(1) Retaliation for break with Soviet policy (2) Destabilize Mao government

TABLE 1.1   **Chronological summary of economic sanctions for foreign policy goals, 1914–83** (*continued*)

Case number	Principal sender	Target country	Active years	Goals of sender country
60-3*	United States	Cuba	1960–	(1) Settle expropriation claims (2) Destabilize Castro government (3) Discourage Cuba from foreign military adventures
61-1*	United States	Ceylon	1961–65	Settle expropriation claims
61-2*	USSR	Albania	1961–82	(1) Retaliation for alliance with China (2) Destabilize Hoxha government
61-3*	NATO Allies	East Germany	1961–62	Berlin Wall
62-1*	United States	Brazil	1962–64	(1) Settle expropriation claims (2) Destabilize Goulart government
62-2*	United Nations	South Africa	1962–	(1) End apartheid (2) Grant independence to Namibia
63-1*	United States	United Arab Republic	1963–65	(1) Cease military activity in Yemen and Congo (2) Moderate anti-US rhetoric
63-2*	Indonesia	Malaysia	1963–67	Promote "Crush Malaysia" campaign
63-3*	United States	Indonesia	1963–66	(1) Cease "Crush Malaysia" campaign (2) Destabilize Sukarno government
63-4	African States	Portugal	1963–65	Leave Africa
65-1*	United States	Chile	1965–66	Roll back copper price

(*continued overleaf*)

TABLE 1.1   **Chronological summary of economic sanctions for foreign policy goals, 1914–83** (*continued*)

Case number	Principal sender	Target country	Active years	Goals of sender country
65-2*	United States	India	1965–67	Alter policy to favor agriculture
65-3*	United Kingdom and United Nations	Rhodesia	1965–79	Majority rule by black Africans
65-4*	United States	Arab League	1965–	Stop US firms from implementing Arab boycott of Israel
65-5	USSR	Romania	1965	Reduce diplomatic openings to the West
67-1	Nigeria	Biafra	1967	End independence movement
68-1	United States	Peru	1968	Forego aircraft purchases from France
68-2*	United States	Peru	1968–74	Settle expropriation claims
68-3	United States	Brazil	1968–69	Restore democracy
70-1*	United States	Chile	1970–73	(1) Settle expropriation claims (2) Destabilize Allende government
71-1*	United States	India and Pakistan	1971	Cease fighting in East Pakistan (Bangladesh)
S-1	United States	Countries Supporting Int'l. Terrorism	1972–	Overview
72-2*	United Kingdom and United States	Uganda	1972–79	(1) Retaliation for expelling Asians (2) Improve human rights (3) Destabilize Amin government
S-2	United States	Countries Violating Human Rights	1973–	Overview

TABLE 1.1   **Chronological summary of economic sanctions for foreign policy goals, 1914–83** (*continued*)

Case number	Principal sender	Target country	Active years	Goals of sender country
73-1*	Arab League	United States and Netherlands	1973–74	(1) Retaliation for supporting Israel in October War (2) Restore pre-1967 Israeli borders
73-2*	United States	South Korea	1973–77	Improve human rights
73-3*	United States	Chile	1973–81	Improve human rights
74-1*	United States	Turkey	1974–78	Withdraw Turkish troops from Cyprus
74-2*	Canada	India	1974–76	(1) Deter further nuclear explosions (2) Apply stricter nuclear safeguards
74-3*	Canada	Pakistan	1974–76	(1) Apply stricter safeguards to nuclear power plant (2) Forego nuclear reprocessing
75-1*	United States and Canada	South Korea	1975–76	Forego nuclear reprocessing
75-2*	United States	USSR	1975–	Liberalize Jewish emigration
75-3*	United States	Eastern Europe	1975–	Liberalize Jewish emigration
75-4*	United States	South Africa	1975–	(1) Adhere to nuclear safeguards (2) Avert explosion of nuclear device
75-5	United States	Cambodia	1975–	(1) Retaliation for North Vietnamese aggression (2) Improve human rights
76-1*	United States	Uruguay	1976–	Improve human rights
76-2*	United States	Taiwan	1976–77	Forego nuclear reprocessing

(*continued overleaf*)

TABLE 1.1   **Chronological summary of economic sanctions for foreign policy goals, 1914–83 (continued)**

Case number	Principal sender	Target country	Active years	Goals of sender country
76-3*	United States	Ethiopia	1976–	(1) Settle expropriation claims (2) Improve human rights
77-1*	United States	Paraguay	1977–	Improve human rights
77-2*	United States	Guatemala	1977–82	Improve human rights
77-3*	United States	Argentina	1977–82	Improve human rights
77-4*	Canada	Japan	1977–78	Adhere to nuclear safeguards
77-5*	United States	Nicaragua	1977–79	(1) Destabilize Somoza government (2) Improve human rights
77-6	United States	El Salvador	1977–81	Improve human rights
78-1*	China	Albania	1978–83	Retaliation for anti-Chinese rhetoric
78-2*	United States	Brazil	1978–80	Adhere to nuclear safeguards
78-3*	United States	Argentina	1978–80	Adhere to nuclear safeguards
78-4*	United States	India	1978–80	Adhere to nuclear safeguards
78-5	United States	USSR	1978–	Liberalize treatment of dissidents (e.g., Sharansky)
78-6	Arab League	Egypt	1978–	Withdraw from Camp David process
78-7	China	Vietnam	1978–	Withdraw troops from Cambodia
78-8*	United States	Libya	1978–	(1) Terminate support of international terrorism (2) Destabilize Qadhafi government
79-1*	United States	Iran	1979–81	(1) Release hostages (2) Settle expropriation claims

TABLE 1.1   **Chronological summary of economic sanctions for foreign policy goals, 1914–83** (*continued*)

Case number	Principal sender	Target country	Active years	Goals of sender country
79-2*	United States	Pakistan	1979–80	Adhere to nuclear safeguards
79-3*	Arab League	Canada	1979–80	Retaliation for planned move of Canadian Embassy in Israel from Tel Aviv to Jerusalem
80-1*	United States	USSR	1980–	(1) Withdraw Soviet troops from Afghanistan (2) Impair Soviet military potential
80-2*	United States	Iraq	1980–82	Terminate support of international terrorism
81-1*	United States	Nicaragua	1981–	(1) End support for El Salvador rebels (2) Destabilize Sandinista government
81-2	USSR	Poland	1981–82	Maintain internal discipline
81-3*	United States	Poland	1981–	(1) Lift martial law (2) Free dissidents (3) Resume talks with Solidarity
81-4*	United States	USSR	1981–82	(1) Lift martial law in Poland (2) Cancel USSR-Europe pipeline project (3) Impair Soviet economic/military potential.
81-6	European Community	Turkey	1981–82	Restore democracy
82-1*	United Kingdom	Argentina	1982	Withdraw troops from Falkland Islands
82-2	Arab League	Zaire	1982	Withdraw recognition of Israel

(*continued overleaf*)

TABLE 1.1   **Chronological summary of economic sanctions for foreign policy goals, 1914–83** (*continued*)

Case number	Principal sender	Target country	Active years	Goals of sender country
82-3*	Netherlands	Suriname	1982–	(1) Improve human rights (2) Limit alliance with Cuba (3) Destabilize Bouterse government
82-4	South Africa	Lesotho	1982–	Return refugees suspected of antistate activities
83-1	Australia	France	1983–	Stop nuclear testing in the South Pacific

* Asterisks denote cases abstracted to date included in the economic and political analysis in this monograph. The abstracts of these and the remaining cases will be published in Gary Clyde Hufbauer, Jeffrey J. Schott, and Kimberly Ann Elliott, *Economic Sanctions Reconsidered: History and Current Policy* (Washington: Institute for International Economics, forthcoming, 1983).

TABLE 1.2   Selected pre-World War I episodes of economic sanctions for foreign policy goals

Sender country	Target country	Active years	Background and objectives	Resolution	Source
Athens	Megara	circa 432 BC	Pericles issued the Megarian decree limiting entry of Megara's products into Athenian markets in retaliation for Megara's attempted expropriation of territory and the kidnapping of three women.	The decree contributed to the Peloponnesian War between Athens and Sparta.	de Ste Croix 252–260; Fornara 222–26
American colonies	Britain	1765	England passed Stamp Act as a revenue measure; colonies boycotted English goods.	Britain repealed the Stamp Act in 1766.	Renwick 5
American colonies	Britain	1767–70	England passed Townshend Acts to cover salaries of judges and officials; colonies boycotted English goods.	Britain repealed the Townshend Acts except on tea; the tea tax gave pretext for the Boston Tea Party of 1774 and calling the Continental Congress.	Renwick 5
Britain France	France Britain	Napoleonic Wars: 1793–1815	British goal: contain French expansion and eventually defeat Napo-	"The experience of economic warfare during this period is inconclusive as to	Jack 1–42

(continued overleaf)

TABLE 1.2   Selected pre-World War I episodes of economic sanctions for foreign policy goals (*continued*)

Sender country	Target country	Active years	Background and objectives	Resolution	Source
			leon; French goal: deprive Britain of grain through the Continental System, and eventually defeat England.	its possible effects when applied with more systematic organization.'' One result of sanctions was French development of beet sugar cultivation, anticipating development of substitutes in later wars.	Knorr 101–2
United States	Britain	1812–14	United States embargoed British goods in response to British Naval Acts limiting US trade with France. The total embargo, which evolved out of the Non-Intercourse Acts of 1809, followed an ineffective embargo imposed from 1807–9.	The Orders in Council which the United States had protested were revoked, but the United States, not knowing of the revocation, declared war two days later. The War of 1812 ensued.	
Britain/France	Russia	Crimean War: 1853–56	Britain and France blockaded the mouth of the Danube River so that the Russian army could not receive supplies by sea.	Russia was defeated and the partition of Turkey prevented.	Oppenheim 514

TABLE 1.2   Selected pre-World War I episodes of economic sanctions for foreign policy goals *(continued)*

Sender country	Target country	Active years	Background and objectives	Resolution	Source
US North	US South	Civil War: 1861–65	"In seapower, railroads, material wealth and industrial capacity to produce iron and munitions the North was vastly superior to the South. This disparity became even more pronounced as the ever tightening blockade gradually cut off the Confederacy from foreign imports."	The South lost: "Attrition and blockade had scuttled the Confederate capacity . . . ."	Leckie 513, Matloff 192
France	Germany	Franco-Prussian War: 1870–71	France declared war on Germany to prevent the emergence of a unified German state. France blockaded the German coast and even occupied German ports in order to prevent supply of German forces.	The German army prevailed despite supply problems.	Dupuy and Dupuy 832

(continued overleaf)

TABLE 1.2   **Selected pre-World War I episodes of economic sanctions for foreign policy goals** (*continued*)

Sender country	Target country	Active years	Background and objectives	Resolution	Source
France	China	Indochina War: 1883–85	At war with China over the Vietnamese territory of Annam, France declared rice to be contraband because of its importance to the Chinese population.	China ceded to France control over the Annamese territory.	Oppenheim 554
United States	Spain	Spanish-American War: 1898	"To the extent the United States had a strategy for conduct of the war against Spain in the Caribbean, it consisted of maintaining a naval blockade of Cuba while native insurgent forces carried on a harassing campaign against Spanish troops on the island." A companion blockade of the Philippines was intended to deny Spain revenues from that colony.	The United States obtained independence for Cuba and, after occupying the Philippines and Puerto Rico, forced Spain to cede those territories and Guam to the United States for $20 million.	Matloff 324–26; Leckie 566
Britain	Dutch South Africa	Boer War: 1899–1902	The British denied articles of contraband to the Boers.	The Boers were eventually overwhelmed and South	Jack 73

TABLE 1.2   Selected pre-World War I episodes of economic sanctions for foreign policy goals (*continued*)

Sender country	Target country	Active years	Background and objectives	Resolution	Source
				Africa added to the British Empire.	
Russia	Japan	Russo-Japanese War: 1904–5	Russia declared rice, all types of fuel, and cotton as contraband.	Following military defeat, Russia ceded portions of its own territory to Japan and recognized Korea as within Japan's sphere of influence.	Oppenheim 454
Italy	Turkey	1911–12	Italy used a limited blockade as part of its campaign to acquire Libya	Italy acquired Libya from the Ottoman Empire.	Dupuy and Dupuy 926

Bibliography, table 1.2.

Dupuy, R. Ernest, and Trevor N. Dupuy. 1970. *The Encyclopedia of Military History*. New York: Harper & Row.

De Ste Croix, G. E. M. 1972. *The Origins of the Peloponnesian War*. London: Duckworth.

Fornara, Charles. 1975. "Plutarch and the Megarian decree." *24 Yale Classical Studies*.

Jack, D. T. 1941. *Studies in Economic Warfare*. New York: Chemical Publishing Co.

Knorr, Klaus. 1977. "International Economic Leverage and its Uses." In Klaus Knorr and Frank N. Traeger, eds. *Economic Issues and National Security*. Lawrence, Kan.: Regent's Press.

Leckie, Robert. 1968. *The Wars of America*. New York: Harper & Row.

Matloff, Maurice, ed. 1969. *American Military History*. Washington: US Government Printing Office.

Oppenheim, L. 1921. "War & Neutrality." In Ronald F. Roxburgh, ed., *International Law: A Treatise*. Vol. II, 3d. ed. London: Longmans, Green & Co.

Renwick, Robin. 1981. *Economic Sanctions*. Harvard Studies in International Affairs No. 45. Cambridge, Mass.: Harvard University Center for International Affairs.

TABLE 1.3   **Comparison of number of sanctions episodes initiated, aggregate cost of sanctions to target countries, and world exports, 1915–83**

Year	Number of episodes initiated in past five years[a]	Aggregate annual cost each fifth year[b] (billion dollars)	Total world exports[c] (billion dollars)
1915	1	0.84	15[d]
1920	2	—	na
1925	2	—	25[e]
1930	0	—	32
1935	3	0.09	na
1940	3	0.76	25[f]
1945	1	0.03	50
1950	9	0.56	55
1955	4	0.65	85
1960	10	1.00	115
1965	14	1.45	165
1970	5	1.26	285
1975	13	1.66	795
1980	22	4.87	1,870

Sources: Tables 1.1 and 4.1 through 4.5 of this monograph; P. Lamartine Yates, *Forty Years of Foreign Trade* (London: George Allen & Unwin, 1959); United Nations, *Yearbook of International Trade Statistics,* various issues; International Monetary Fund, *International Financial Statistics,* various issues.

a. The counts are based on table 1.1; the figure for 1975, for example, represents cases initiated in 1971, 1972, 1973, 1974, and 1975.

b. The figures represent the annualized cost to target countries of outstanding cases, based on abstracts of 78 cases summarized in Tables 4.1 through 4.5. All figures are in current dollars, rounded to the nearest $10 million.

c. Based on P. Lamartine Yates for 1915 to 1940; UN for 1945; *International Financial Statistics* for 1950 to 1983. All figures are in current dollars, rounded to the nearest $5 billion.

d. Extrapolated from 1913 data ($21.0 billion).

e. Estimated from average of 1926–29 data ($31.6 billion).

f. Extrapolated from 1938 data ($22.7 billion).

2 Anatomy of a Sanctions Episode

The case abstracts we have compiled provide the data base for our analysis. The abstracts will be published in our forthcoming book, *Economic Sanctions Reconsidered: History and Current Policy*. The narrative portion of each abstract sets out what happened and—in the view of actual participants and case historians—why. Each abstract also contains statistical information on the economy of the target country and economic relations between the target and sender countries. This information underlies our evaluation of motives and outcomes.

This chapter describes our definitions and methods. It may be skipped by readers who are eager to turn to the results.

Senders and Targets

We use the term "sender" to designate the principal author of the sanctions episode. More than one country may be engaged in the campaign, but usually a single country takes the lead and brings others along. The leader may enlist support through bilateral consultations or, less frequently, through an international organization—the League of Nations, the United Nations, or the Organization of American States. In a few instances, two countries, or a country and an international organization, may share leadership, and in these cases both are listed as "sender countries" in table 1.1. Our abstracts concentrate on the motives and actions of the sender country, with separate mention made of the supporting cast.

We use the term "target" to describe the immediate object of the episode. On occasion, sanctions may be aimed at two or more countries, for example, the COCOM sanctions directed against the USSR and its East European allies. The lessons of a sanctions episode can also be intended for countries that might be silently contemplating objectionable policies, for example, imprisoning political opponents, undertaking a nuclear weapons program, or embarking on a military adventure. However, our abstracts and analysis necessarily concentrate on the response of the immediate targets.

Type of Sanctions

There are three main ways a sender country tries to inflict costs on the target country: first by limiting exports; second by restricting imports; third by impeding finance, including the reduction of aid. Most of the cases we have studied involve some interruption of trade. Such measures engender costs to the target country in terms of lost export markets, denial of critical imports, lower prices received for embargoed exports, and higher prices paid for substitute imports.

In over half of the cases, both export and import controls have been employed. In instances where only one or the other is invoked, export controls are almost always preferred to restrictions on imports. Exports have been manipulated in such highly publicized cases as the Arab oil embargo of 1973–74 and President Carter's cutoff of grain shipments to the USSR. One of the few examples of the use of import controls alone was the USSR embargo on wool imports from Australia in 1954 in an unsuccessful attempt to force the return of a defected Soviet diplomat.

Why have import controls been used less often? There seem to be two explanations: first, target countries usually can find alternative markets or arrange triangular purchase arrangements to circumvent import controls. Indeed, for many products—especially bulk commodities such as oil and grains—it is hard to verify the origin of the goods entering customs. Secondly, some important sender countries do not have the legal authority to impose import controls for foreign policy reasons. The United States, for example, can impose import limitations pursuant to a national security finding or a presidential declaration of national emergency under section 232 of the Trade Expansion Act of 1962 or under the International Emergency Economic Powers Act. Both avenues are unwieldy administratively; as a result, the United States rarely has imposed import sanctions, the most notable cases being against Iran and Libya (for oil imports), pursuant to a 1975 national security finding under section 232.

Target countries are often hurt through the interruption of commercial and official finance. The interruption of commercial finance will usually require the target country to pay a higher interest rate to alternative creditors. The same happens when official finance is turned off. In addition, when a poor country is the target, the grant component of official financing often provides further leverage. The United States, for example, manipulated food aid in the 1960s to great effect with the United Arab Republic, India, and Chile, and used the carrot-and-stick approach with military aid in the 1970s, improving the human rights situation in South Korea, but failing to move Turkey out of Cyprus.

The ultimate form of financial and trade control is a freeze of the target country's assets. A freeze not only stops financial flows; it also directly and indirectly impedes trade. The US freeze of Iranian assets in late 1979 played an important role in the eventual resolution of the hostage crisis. The UK freeze of Argentine assets made a modest contribution to the British victory in the Falklands in 1982.

Foreign Policy Goals

We have found it useful to divide the episodes into five categories, classified according to the major foreign policy objective sought by the sender country. The following letter key is used in the tables accompanying chapter 3:

A. Change target country policies in a relatively modest way (modest in the scale of national goals, but often of burning importance to participants in the episode), illustrated by the human rights and nuclear nonproliferation cases.

B. Destabilize the target government (including, as an ancillary goal, change the target country policies), illustrated by the US campaign against Castro, and the Soviet campaign against Tito.

C. Disrupt a minor military adventure, illustrated by the UK sanctions against Argentina over the Falkland Islands.

D. Impair the military potential of the target country, illustrated by World Wars I and II and the COCOM sanctions against the USSR and its allies.

E. Change target country policies in a major way (including the surrender of territory), illustrated by the UN campaign against South Africa over apartheid and control of Namibia.

An episode may have more than one objective. Such cases are classified according to the most difficult objective, except in a few instances where two objectives are judged to be equally elusive; in those few instances the cases are cross-listed. For example, in the US campaign against Cuba, the principal objective shifted from settlement of expropriation claims, to destabilization, to an attempt to disrupt military adventurism. Destabilization usually presupposes a lesser goal, in this instance settlement of the expropriation dispute. Hence, we submerge the expropriation dispute within the destabilization category. However, we cross list the *United States v. Cuba* case as a disruption of military adventure case as well as a destabilization episode because both objectives seemed equally elusive.

Other examples of multiple policy goals are the cases of *United States v. Argentina* (1944–1947: Peron) and *United States v. Laos* (1956–1962: prevent communist takeover). In the Argentine case, the United States was initially preoccupied with ending the love affair between Argentina and fascism; later senior US officials began to view Juan Perón as an exponent of fascism and therefore a target for removal from office. We have listed this case solely as a destabilization episode, although it had another important goal, namely ridding Argentina of fascist tendencies. In the Laos case, the United States was preoccupied with purging Laos of communist tendencies. In pursuit of this elusive goal, the United States first destabilized the government of the left-leaning Prince Souvanna Phouma, and then, a few years later, destabilized the government of his right-leaning successor, General Phoumi. Again, we have listed this case solely as a destabilization episode. To summarize our method of classification: a destabilization episode usually encompasses either modest policy goals (category A) or other major changes in target country policies (category E), but it is not cross-listed under these headings. However, a destabilization case that also entails disruption of a minor military adventure (a fairly infrequent overlap) is listed under both categories.

Attempts to impair the military power of an adversary usually encompass an explicit or implicit goal—however elusive—of destabilizing the target country's government. Hence, we list these cases only under the impairment heading (category D).

Sender countries do not always announce their goals with clarity. Indeed, obfuscation is the rule in destabilization cases. The USSR never directly said it wished to overthrow Tito or Hoxha; the United States was equally circumspect in its public statements about Castro, Allende, and the Sandinistas. Moreover, goals may change during the course of an episode. Here, as elsewhere in this study, we must rely on newspaper accounts and other secondary sources in assigning episodes to categories.

Overview of the Variables

Whether to impose sanctions—and if so, how—is influenced by a whole host of factors, both domestic and international, which constrain the actions a sender country can take in pursuit of its foreign policy goals. For example, conflicting pressures within the sender government often lead to an indecisive response, which neither sends the desired political signal nor imposes arduous costs on the target country.

The classic example of confused signals was the League of Nations sanctions against Italy in 1935–36 (see appendix A). The major powers in the League (Britain and France) were torn between their desire to stop the Italian advance in Abyssinia and their fear of upsetting the political balance in Europe. With an eye on upcoming national elections, efforts were made to keep the peace in Europe; thus, even while sanctions were being considered by the League Council, attempts were made to appease the Italians by ceding some territory in Abyssinia.

Clearly, there are a number of underlying elements that may influence the outcome of a sanctions episode. The factors that influence a specific episode are described in the abstracts of each case. We have divided these, somewhat artificially, into two clusters: a group of "political" variables and a group of "economic" variables. The political variables that we have scored (by no means an exhaustive list) include:

- companion policies used by the sender country, namely covert maneuvers (identified by a J), quasi-military activity (identified by a Q), and regular military activity (identified by an R)

- the number of years economic sanctions were in force

- the extent of international cooperation in imposing sanctions, scaled from 1 (no cooperation) to 4 (significant cooperation)

- the political stability and economic health of the target country, scaled from 1 (a distressed country) to 3 (a strong and stable country).

The economic variables that we have scored (again not an exhaustive list) include:

- the cost imposed on the target country, expressed in absolute terms, and as a percentage of its gross national product (GNP)

- commercial relations between the sender and target countries, measured by the flow of trade between them as a percentage of the target country's total trade

- the respective economic size of the countries, measured by the ratio of their GNP values

- the type of sanctions, namely whether it involved an interruption of finance (identified by an F), an interruption of exports from the sender country (identified by an X), or an interruption of imports to the sender country (identified by an M)

- the cost to the sender country, expressed as an index scaled from 1 (net gain to sender) to 4 (major loss to sender).

In this chapter, we describe our approach to distilling and quantifying "success," and then discuss each of the underlying political and economic variables. In chapter 3, we discuss the connection between success and political variables. In chapter 4, we examine the relationship between success and economic variables. Finally, in chapter 5, we summarize our findings and draw policy conclusions.

The Success of an Episode

The "success" of an economic sanctions episode—as viewed from the perspective of the sender country—has two parts: the extent to which the policy outcome sought by the sender country was in fact achieved, and the contribution made by sanctions to a positive outcome. In determining whether the episode was "successful," we confine our examination to changes in the policies, capabilities or government of the target country.

Our standard of success is whether the sanctions contributed to the achievement of the *stated* foreign policy goals of the sender country. As noted earlier, domestic political motives may overshadow concerns about changing foreign behavior. Unfortunately, the literature on individual economic sanctions episodes seldom evaluates the role of domestic political objectives or indicates whether they were satisfied.

Our conclusions regarding both the achievement of the foreign policy goals and the contribution of sanctions to the outcome are heavily influenced by the qualitative conclusions reached by previous scholars of the particular episodes, as summarized in the abstracts. We recognize that such assessments entail a good deal of subjective evaluation. Indeed, since foreign policy objectives often come in multiple parts, since objectives evolve over time, and since the contribution of sanctions to the policy outcome is often murky, judgment plays an important role in assigning a single number to each element of the "success equation." However, by relying on the consensus views of other analysts of the cases, we believe we have minimized the bias resulting from our personal views.

We have devised a simple index system, scaled from 1 to 4, to score each element. Our index system is described as follows:

Policy Result

(1) failed outcome, illustrated by the USSR attempt to destabilize Tito in the period 1948–55

(2) unclear but possibly positive outcome, illustrated by the Arab League's long campaign against Israel which, to some extent, has isolated Israel in the international community

(3) positive outcome, that is to say, a somewhat successful result, illustrated by US efforts to prevent a communist takeover of the Laotian government during the period 1956–62

(4) successful outcome, illustrated by the joint efforts of the United Kingdom and United States to overthrow Idi Amin in Uganda in the late 1970s.

Sanctions Contribution

(1) zero or negative contribution, illustrated by the US campaign against Ethiopia from 1976 to the present

(2) minor contribution, illustrated by the USSR withdrawal of assistance from China in the 1960s

(3) modest contribution, illustrated by the withdrawal of Dutch economic aid to Suriname since 1982

(4) significant contribution, illustrated by the US success in destabilizing the Trujillo government in the Dominican Republic in 1960–61.

By multiplication, the two elements are combined into a "success score" that ranges in value from 1 to 16. We characterize a score of 9 or higher as a "successful" outcome. Successful does not mean that the target country was vanquished by the denial of economic contacts or even that the sanctions decisively influenced the outcome. Success is defined against more modest standards. A score of 9 means that sanctions made a modest contribution to the goal sought by the sender country and that the goal was in part realized; a score of 16 means that sanctions made a significant contribution to a successful outcome. By contrast, a score of 1 indicates that the sender country clearly failed to achieve its goals; indeed sanctions may even have left the sender country worse off than before the measures were imposed.

Companion Policy Measures

"War is nothing but the continuation of politics with the admixture of other means."[1] The same could be said of economic sanctions. Indeed, sanctions frequently serve as a junior weapon in a battery of diplomatic artillery aimed at the antagonistic state. Leaving aside the normal means of diplomatic protest—exemplified by recalling an ambassador or cancelling a cultural mission—we distinguish three types of companion policies: covert action; quasi-military action; and regular military action.

Covert action, mounted by the intelligence forces, often accompanies the imposition of economic sanctions when the destabilization of a target government is sought. In destabilization cases and in other episodes where major policy changes are sought, the sender state may invoke quasi-military force—for example, massing troops at the border, or stationing war vessels off the coast. Finally, sanctions may precede or accompany armed hostility.

Length of Sanctions

The life of a sanctions episode is not often defined with the precision of college matriculation and graduation. In the early phases, the sender country may take pains to conceal and even deny that it is imposing sanctions. This seems to have been the case when the United States first began its campaigns against Chile in 1970 and against Nicaragua in 1981. In other cases, the whole episode may pass with hardly an official word, as in the US actions against the United Kingdom and France in the Suez episode of 1956. In still other cases, the ending may be misty rather than sharp, as in the USSR campaigns against Albania and China.

Our approach in dating episodes is to start the episode with the first recorded sanctions threat from official sources or the first recorded sanctions event—whichever comes earlier. We stop the episode when the sender or target country changes its policies in a significant way, or when the campaign

---

1. Carl von Clausewitz, *Vom Kriege* (1832), cited in *The Oxford Dictionary of Quotations*, 3d ed. (Oxford: Oxford University Press, 1979), p. 152.

simply withers away. Because exact dates of the onset and termination of sanctions episodes are often indistinct, we have made an arbitrary decision to calculate the length of sanctions episodes by rounding to the nearest whole year, disregarding the beginning and ending month, with a minimum of one year. For example, an episode that began in January 1981 and ended in November 1983 would be counted as lasting two years (1983 *minus* 1981 *equals* 2).

International Cooperation

In high profile cases, such as the two world wars, the League of Nations foray against Italy, and the series of US sanctions against the USSR, much emphasis has been placed on achieving international cooperation in order to deny the target country the supplies or markets of its principal trading partners. In fact, the degree of cooperation realized has usually disappointed the lead country. Even in World Wars I and II, when the Allies ultimately achieved a high degree of cooperation, Germany was able to draw on supplies from Eastern Europe and adjacent neutral powers. The following statement, taken not from a lament of President Reagan's advisors at the Versailles or Williamsburg summits, but from a commentary on World War I, describes the problem:[2]

. . . all attempts in this direction [of a permanent inter-Allied organization] had been wrecked by the contradictory nature of the commercial interests of the Allied nations, which were only kept in touch with one another by means of intermittent conferences . . . .

Nevertheless, while a complete economic blockade is seldom achieved, there are substantial differences in the degree of cooperation realized. We have used an index scaled from 1 to 4 to grade the extent of cooperation:

(1) no cooperation: a single sender country imposes sanctions, and usually seeks no cooperation; illustrated by the *United States v. Brazil* (1962–64: Goulart)

(2) minor cooperation: the sender country enlists verbal support and possibly token restraints from other countries; illustrated by the *United States v. Poland* (1981–   : martial law)

---

2. Louis Guichard, *The Naval Blockade, 1914–1918* (New York: Appleton, 1930), p. 67.

(3)   modest cooperation: the sender country obtains meaningful restraints—but limited in time and coverage—from some but not all the important trading partners of the target country, illustrated by the *United States v. Cuba* (1960–   : Castro) and *United Kingdom and United Nations v. Rhodesia* (1965–79: black majority rule)

(4)   significant cooperation: the important trading partners make a major effort to limit trade, although leakages may still exist through neutral countries, illustrated by the two world wars, and the early years of COCOM and CHINCOM.

The many efforts and inevitable failures in building watertight economic barriers have led, we think, to an overemphasis on the role played by cooperation in determining the success or failure of a sanctions episode. Proponents of economic sanctions often engage in an "if only" form of argument.[3] "If only" the Europeans and the United States would impose a financial freeze on Argentina. "If only" the United States would halt all trade with South Africa. "If only" the Europeans would restrict their commerce with the Soviet Union.

From the standpoint of the sender country, it is almost axiomatic that more cooperation is better than less. But other variables are also at play. A critical variable is the nature of the objective. The inspiring words of Browning seem written for sender countries: "A man's reach should exceed his grasp, or what's a heaven for?" The pursuit of more ambitious objectives accompanied by much fanfare often goes hand in hand with efforts to enlist international cooperation. After all, other countries are not likely to rally in support of modest goals; and the grasp of ambitious objectives usually remains beyond the reach of sender countries, even when those countries are assisted by a large measure of international cooperation.

Economic Health and Political Stability

The atmosphere in the target country is critical to the outcome of a sanctions episode. An analogy with rainmaking is appropriate. If storm clouds are overhead, rain may fall without man's help. If moisture-laden clouds are in

---

3. As an example of the "if only" argument in the Rhodesian context, see C. Lloyd Brown-John, *Multilateral Sanctions in International Law: A Comparative Analysis* (New York: Praeger, 1975), p. 378.

the sky, chemical seeding may bring forth rain. If the skies are clear and dry, no amount of human assistance will produce rain. Similarly, sanctions may be redundant, productive, or useless in pursuing foreign policy goals depending on the economic health and political stability of the target country.

It is no simple matter to summarize the complex of events that describe a country's economy and politics at a point in time. Our task is made more difficult because we wish to know the target country's health and stability in the absence of sanctions over a period of time. Consider, for example, the problem of assessing health and stability in the context of a successful destabilization case. At the beginning of the episode, the target country might be experiencing significant problems; shortly before its downfall, the target government might well have reached a crisis stage, quite apart from the pressure imposed as a result of sanctions. We have heroically put these difficulties to one side in devising an index with values of 1, 2, and 3 to describe the overall political and economic health of the target country, throughout the period of the sanctions episode, and in the hypothetical absence of sanctions:

(1) distress: a country with acute economic problems, exemplified by high unemployment and rampant inflation, coupled with political turmoil bordering on chaos, illustrated by Chile at the time of Allende and Uganda in the later years of the Amin regime

(2) significant problems: a country with severe economic problems, such as a foreign exchange crisis, coupled with substantial internal dissent, illustrated by Ceylon under P.M. Bandaranaike

(3) strong and stable: a country with the government in firm control (even though dissent may be present) and an economy experiencing only the normal range of inflation, unemployment and similar ills, illustrated by India during the nuclear nonproliferation campaigns of the 1970s and the USSR at the time of the Afghanistan invasion.

Estimating the Costs

Sanctions are designed to penalize the target country for its unwanted behavior. In theory, the target country will weigh the costs imposed by the sanctions against the benefits derived from its continuing policies—the higher the cost, the more likely that the target country will alter its policies. The cost that sanctions impose on a target country cannot, however, be viewed as an abstract number: a cost of $100 million means more to Chile than to the USSR. We have, therefore, related the cost figures to the gross national product of the target country. Our methodology for estimating the cost to the target country is explained in detail in appendix B.

We have not attempted to calculate the actual costs of sanctions to sender countries. Instead, we have drawn from the case abstracts a rough sense of the trade or financial loss incurred by the sender from the imposition of sanctions, and have related this loss to the sender country's total external trade. Illustrations of our approach are provided in chapter 4. The following index reflects our judgment as to the relative cost to the sender country:

(1) net gain to sender: usually cases where aid is withheld, illustrated by the US suspension of aid to Turkey in 1974

(2) little effect on sender: cases where a trivial dislocation occurs, illustrated by the US export controls on nuclear fuel shipments to Taiwan in 1976

(3) modest loss to sender: some trade is lost, but neither the size nor the concentration of the loss is substantial, illustrated by the League of Nations campaign against Italy in 1935–36

(4) major loss to sender: large volumes of trade are adversely affected, illustrated by the two world wars against Germany.

Country Size and Trade Links

Quite apart from the magnitude of costs that the sender imposes on the target, the outcome of a sanctions episode may be influenced by the relative size of the two countries and the trade links between them. The imposition of even minor sanctions carries the implicit threat of more drastic action. Whether that threat looms large or small depends very much on respective country sizes and trade flows. Hence, we include among our economic variables a ratio between sender country and target country GNP levels, and figures on trade between target and sender expressed as a percentage of the target country's total trade.

Analytic Methods

In this monograph, we focus on relations between individual explanatory variables and the outcomes—successful or otherwise—of the various groups of episodes. In addition, we have performed exploratory multiple regression analysis, relating the case success scores to all the variables simultaneously. The full multiple regression results will be set forth in our forthcoming book. However, the exploratory work suggests that the multiple regression coefficients are generally consistent with the findings summarized here. One significant inconsistency between the variable-by-variable analysis and the multiple regression analysis is noted in chapter 4.

On to the Results

With these methodological issues out of the way, the road is now clear for us to examine "success" in terms of the underlying political and economic variables.

3   Political Variables

In evaluating "success," the first step is to distinguish between types of foreign policy objectives sought in different sanctions episodes. The nature of the objective may be the most important political variable of all: sanctions cannot stop a military assault as easily as they can free a political prisoner. Accordingly, our discussion is organized around five major groups of objectives, namely: modest changes in policy, destabilization of the target government, disruption of military adventures, impairment of military potential, and other major policy changes. As mentioned in chapter 2, in classifying cases the more ambitious goal takes precedence over the less ambitious goal. Thus, destabilization cases usually involve, as ancillary goals, the search for modest or even major policy changes. Only occasionally are cases cross-listed under two objectives.

Modest Changes in Policy

Sanctions have been frequently threatened or deployed in pursuit of relatively modest changes in the policies of target countries. Modest changes are not trivial changes. At the time, changes that we have labeled "modest" may have seemed overwhelmingly important to the target or sender country. But in the grander scale of events, the settlement of an expropriation dispute, or the improvement of human rights on a limited scale, does not compare with stopping a military adventure or destabilizing a government.

Illustrative of these episodes is the case of *United States and Canada v. South Korea* (1975–76), where South Korea was dissuaded from procuring a nuclear reprocessing plant from France as a result of the threat of financial sanctions from the US and Canada. The objective was quite specific, and the sender states had a great deal of leverage due to Korea's "sensitivity . . . to a slight hardening in Canadian and American financial terms [for nuclear transactions]."[1]

The United States is particularly active in the pursuit of modest policy goals cases, accounting for 24 of the 31 cases listed in table 3.1. This

---

1. Albert Wohlstetter, "Spreading the Bomb Without Quite Breaking the Rules," 25 *Foreign Policy* (Winter 1976/1977), p. 168.

lopsided US weight may partly reflect our omission of contests between second- and third-rank powers over modest policy goals.

Of the 31 modest change cases listed in table 3.1, there are some 18 cases where we scored the outcome as positive (score 3) or successful (score 4). (All tables appear at the end of this chapter.) In 20 of 31 cases, we conclude that sanctions made a contribution to the outcome ranging from modest (score 3) to significant (score 4). The combined result is that, in 15 of the 31 cases, we obtain a success score of 9 or higher. Thus, by our analysis, in almost half of the modest policy change cases, the sender country made some progress in achieving its goals through the use of economic sanctions. This, we think, is a significant finding. As often as not, the pursuit of modest goals with economic sanctions is likely to be rewarded with at least modest success—a far better batting average than the current wave of skepticism might suggest.

In their quest for modest policy changes, sender countries usually do not employ covert force, neither do they engage in quasi-military measures, or regular military action. Rather, in this group of cases, sanctions tend to stand alone as the policy instrument.

International cooperation was generally minor or nonexistent in the group of modest policy change cases. Indeed, it was usually not sought. A look at table 3.1 reveals that there is little correlation between the extent of international cooperation and the contribution of sanctions to the policy outcome.

In the 15 cases for which the success score was 9 or higher, the average sanctions period was 3.4 years. In the 16 cases with success scores of 8 or lower, the average sanctions period was 4.6 years, and in 8 of these unsuccessful cases, sanctions are still in effect. Shorter is better.

The average score for the economic health and political stability of the target country in successful cases was 2.2. By comparison, the health and stability score in less successful episodes was 2.4. Evidently, better health contributes in part to greater resistance.

Destabilizing a Government

Destabilization episodes usually spring from conflicts over other issues. In some instances, the underlying dispute involves modest changes in target country policies, for example expropriation (*United States v. Brazil*, 1962–64), terrorism (*United States v. Libya*, 1978–   ), or human rights (*Netherlands v. Suriname*, 1982–   ). In other instances, destabilization is sought because the target government has adopted a hostile attitude in its overall relations with the sender country. This category of cases has a decided East–West flavor—for example, in episodes involving Yugoslavia, Finland, and Albania, the USSR found its smaller allies wandering from the socialist sphere; in cases involving Cuba, Brazil, and Chile, the United States found its neighbors stealing away from the capitalist camp. When another goal underlies or accompanies a destabilization case, we have generally listed these cases only in the destabilization group. We make an exception, however, when the sender country seeks both to destabilize a government and to disrupt a military adventure; such cases are cross-listed under both headings.

Table 3.2 summarizes 18 destabilization cases. Our research suggests that sanctions, coupled with other policies, are surprisingly successful in destabilizing governments. In half of the destabilization cases, the success score is 9 or greater, and in 3 of the remaining cases (*United States v. Libya, 1978– ; United States v. Nicaragua, 1981– ; and Netherlands v. Suriname, 1982–*) the outcome remains in doubt. This high success rate contrasts sharply with the skepticism expressed in the literature, and compares positively with results obtained in applying sanctions to obtain other foreign policy goals.

A word of caution: it must be emphasized that economic sanctions seldom achieve destabilization unassisted by companion measures. Covert action and quasi-military operations regularly play a role in destabilization cases; indeed, companion policies were present in all but three of the episodes. On the other hand, international cooperation is not an important ingredient of successful destabilization episodes. In two cases the Soviet Union was supported by its East European allies; and the United States enjoyed some international cooperation in its efforts to isolate Cuba. But in each of these instances the target country received considerable material and moral support from an opposing major power, which compensated for the impact of the sanctions on the target country and led to low success scores.

In the nine cases with a success score of 9 or higher the average sanctions period was 4.3 years; in the nine other cases (including two which are still open, *United States v. Nicaragua, 1981– ; and Netherlands v. Suriname, 1982–*) the average sanctions period was 7.4 years. Sanctions that have an immediate impact are those that are most effective. If an episode drags on, this probably indicates that the objective was more difficult to achieve; moreover countervailing forces can arise to blunt the effect of the sanctions and block attainment of the sender's foreign policy goals.

The average index of economic health and political stability for target governments that succumbed to destabilization was only 1.4. By contrast, the average index for target regimes that resisted destabilization was 2.1. Prosaic but true: governments in distress are more easily destabilized.

Disrupting Military Adventures

At the end of World War I the classic rationale offered for economic sanctions was to persuade hostile countries to abandon their military adventures. Lord Curzon, speaking in 1918, suggested that the sure application of sanctions might have averted the outbreak of a lesser conflict than World War I:[2]

[Sanctions] did not, it is true, succeed in preventing the war; they have not, at any rate at present curtailed its duration, but I should like to put it this way. I doubt very much whether, if Germany had anticipated when she plunged into war the consequences, commercial, financial, and otherwise, which would be entailed upon her by two, three, or four years of war, she would not have been eager to plunge in as she was. Remember this. Though possibly we have not done all we desired, we have done a great deal, and we could have done a great deal more if our hands had not been tied by certain difficulties. It is naturally a delicate matter for me to allude to this. A good many of them have been removed by the entry of the United States of America into the war, but we have always the task of handling with great and necessary delicacy the neutral states, and this difficulty still remains with us.

Apparently influenced by the arguments of spokesmen such as Lord Curzon and President Wilson, British and American policy officials have increasingly used sanctions as an explicit substitute for military action or as a key component of an overall effort to disrupt unwelcome military adventures.

Table 3.3 identifies 15 military adventure cases. We define a military adventure as an action on a less grand scale than the Napoleonic Wars or the two world wars. The classic instance is the *League of Nations v. Italy* (1935–36); other instances include *United States v. Japan* (1940–41); *United States v. Cuba* (1960–   ); and *United Kingdom v. Argentina* (1982). There are few ambiguous cases in this group: when sanctions succeeded, they did so decisively; when they failed, they flopped. In 6 of these cases, a success score of 9 or higher was reached. In the remaining 9 cases, sanctions failed to deter the target country's martial ambitions.

---

2. D. Mitrany, *The Problem of International Sanctions* (London: Oxford University Press, 1925), p. 36.

The presence of companion measures—covert interference and military and quasi-military action—was not decisive in distinguishing between success and failure cases. In only one case, *United Kingdom v. Argentina* (1982), were companion policies used to good effect. But in five other instances, companion policies did not materially advance the desired outcome.

International cooperation, if anything, made a perverse difference. The average degree of cooperation in the six success cases was 1.8; the average degree of cooperation in the nine failure cases was 2.4. In the success episodes, the sanctions period on average lasted 1.2 years. In the failure episodes, the average sanctions period was 4.6 years (excluding the everlasting Cuban case, the average failed episode spanned 2.2 years).

Target countries that engage in military adventures are usually not in acute distress. At most they have significant internal problems—for example, malfunctioning economies in Egypt in the mid-1970s and in Turkey in 1974. However, the weaker the national condition, the more likely that sanctions will succeed. The average health and stability index for target countries was 2.0 in success cases and 2.6 in failure cases.

An additional feature that helps distinguish between success and failure episodes was not listed in table 3.3. Success more often (but not invariably) resulted when the target country was either an ally or at least on friendly terms with the sender country prior to the episode: *League of Nations v. Greece* (1925); *United States v. Netherlands* (1948–49); *United States v. United Arab Republic* (1963–65). By contrast, in cases where a background of hostility preceded the use of sanctions, success proved elusive: *United States v. Japan* (1940–41); *United States/CHINCOM v. China* (1949–70); *United States v. Cuba* (1960–   ); *United States v. USSR* (1980–   ).

Impairing Military Potential

The immediate purpose of practically every economic sanctions episode is to diminish the potential of the target country. Nevertheless, we can distinguish between the imposition of short-term economic measures to achieve defined political goals, and the conduct of a long-term campaign to weaken an adversary that poses a broad threat to the sender country. Table 3.4 lists eight episodes where weakening the target's economy became an end in its own right. These episodes usually involve contests between major powers, often in wartime or in the shadow of war.

In neither World War I nor II, nor in the Korean War, did the Allies believe that sanctions would decisively contribute to the outcome. Instead, they hoped and expected that economic denial would marginally limit the adversary's military capabilities. Economic sanctions became a minor adjunct to a major war effort, and "trading with the enemy" was labeled an offense in its own right, quite apart from calculations of cost and benefit. These features distinguish the impairment episodes from the disruption of military adventure cases. Similarly, for more than three decades, the United States has sought to limit the economic underpinnings of the Soviet military machine, initially through COCOM, and more recently through denial measures associated with the Afghanistan invasion and the Polish crisis.

Apart from the two world wars, we assign these episodes low success scores. Without exception, the target countries are economically healthy and politically stable. With the exception of Israel, the targets are major powers. It is unreasonable to expect that sanctions that involve a relatively modest quantity of goods or finance can significantly detract from the economic strength of a major power.

It is not surprising that the two successes were associated with major wars. Even in wartime, as subsequent studies of defeated Germany showed, there were few key links in the economy which—even when destroyed by sanctions or by bombing—decisively crippled the war machine. Instead, the contribution of sanctions was a contribution of attrition.

Other Major Policy Changes

Under this heading, we put cases that are not already covered by the destabilization and impairment groupings. Examples include the *United Nations v. South Africa* (1962–   ), over apartheid and Namibia); and the *Arab League v. United States and Netherlands* (1973–74, over support of Israel).

As table 3.5 shows, in only 1 of the 11 cases was a success score of even 9 reached. The borderline success case was the *Arab League v. United States and Netherlands*. The sudden rise in the price of oil in 1973–74 from $2.59/bbl. to $11.65/bbl. gave the Organization of Petroleum Exporting Countries (OPEC) instant and spectacular wealth. In our judgment, the sanctions were more an occasion than a cause of the price leap. However, the threat to withhold oil from diplomatic adversaries contributed to a shift in West European and Japanese policies on the Palestinian question. Accordingly, we conclude that sanctions made a positive contribution to the diplomatic achievements of the OPEC group, although we recognize that other observers might ascribe to sanctions a less important role.

To mention just a few of the failures, there is no evidence that UN sanctions have materially affected South African attitudes on apartheid, or that the Arab League boycott has moved Israel on the question of establishing a Palestinian homeland, or that sanctions helped Indonesia acquire the territory occupied by Malaysia. It is noteworthy that the target countries in this group generally enjoy the highest level of economic health and political stability, and that the failure cases on average lasted 8.6 years.

TABLE 3.1 Modest changes in target country policies: political variables

Case[a]	Sender and target	Policy result[b] (index)	Sanctions contri- bution[c] (index)	Success score[d] (index)	Companion policies[e]	International cooperation[f] (index)	Sanctions period[g] (years)	Health and stability[h] (index)	Other goals[i]
33-1	UK v. USSR	4	3	12	—	1	1	2	—
38-1	US/UK v. Mexico	3	3	9	—	2	9	3	—
54-1	USSR v. Australia	1	1	1	—	1	1	3	—
61-1	US v. Ceylon	4	4	16	—	1	4	2	—
63-1	US v. UAR	4	4	16	—	1	2	2	C
65-1	US v. Chile	3	4	12	—	1	1	2	—
65-2	US v. India	4	4	16	—	1	2	2	—
68-2	US v. Peru	4	4	16	—	1	6	2	—
73-2	US v. S. Korea	3	4	12	—	1	4	2	—
73-3	US v. Chile	3	3	9	—	1	8	1	—
74-2	Canada v. India	2	3	6	—	2	2	3	—
74-3	Canada v. Pakistan	2	2	4	—	2	2	2	—
75-1	US/Canada v. S. Korea	4	4	16	—	2	1	3	—
75-2	US v. USSR	2	2	4	—	1	8+	3	—
75-3	US v. Eastern Europe	3	4	12	—	1	8+	3	—
75-4	US v. S. Africa	2	2	4	—	2	8+	3	—
76-1	US v. Uruguay	3	2	6	—	1	7+	2	—
76-2	US v. Taiwan	4	4	16	—	2	1	2	—
76-3	US v. Ethiopia	1	1	1	—	2	7+	1	—
77-1	US v. Paraguay	2	3	6	—	1	6+	3	—
77-2	US v. Guatemala	2	2	4	—	1	5	2	—

(continued overleaf)

TABLE 3.1   Modest changes in target country policies: political variables (*continued*)

Case[a]	Sender and target	Policy result[b] (index)	Sanctions contribution[c] (index)	Success score[d] (index)	Companion policies[e]	International cooperation[f] (index)	Sanctions period[g] (years)	Health and stability[h] (index)	Other goals[i]
77-3	US v. Argentina	3	2	6	—	1	5	2	—
77-4	Canada v. Japan	4	4	16	—	1	1	3	—
78-1	China v. Albania	1	1	1	—	1	5	3	—
78-2	US v. Brazil	2	3	6	—	2	5+	2	—
78-3	US v. Argentina	2	3	6	—	2	5+	2	—
78-4	US v. India	2	3	6	—	2	5+	3	—
79-1	US v. Iran	4	3	12	Q	2	2	1	—
79-2	US v. Pakistan	3	2	6	—	2	1	2	—
79-3	Arab League v. Canada	4	3	12	—	2	1	3	—
80-2	US v. Iraq	2	2	4	—	1	2	2	—

Notes: See table 3.5.

TABLE 3.2 Destabilization of target governments: political variables

Case[a]	Sender and target	Policy result[b] (index)	Sanctions contribution[c] (index)	Success score[d] (index)	Companion policies[e]	International cooperation[f] (index)	Sanctions period[g] (years)	Health and stability[h] (index)	Other goals[i]
18-1	UK v. Russia	1	1	1	Q,R	4	2	1	—
44-1	US v. Argentina	2	2	4	—	1	3	2	—
48-4	USSR v. Yugoslavia	1	1	1	Q	4	7	3	—
51-1	UK/US v. Iran	4	3	12	J	2	2	2	—
56-4	US v. Laos	3	3	9	—	2	6	1	—
58-1	USSR v. Finland	4	4	16	—	1	1	3	—
60-1	US v. Dominican Republic	4	4	16	Q	3	2	1	—
60-3	US v. Cuba	1	1	1	Q,J	3	23+	2	C
61-2	USSR v. Albania	1	1	1	Q	4	21	3	—
62-1	US v. Brazil	4	3	12	J	1	2	1	—
63-3	US v. Indonesia	4	2	8	J	1	3	2	C
65-3	UK/UN v. Rhodesia	4	3	12	Q	4	14	2	—
70-1	US v. Chile	4	3	12	J	1	3	1	—
72-2	UK/US v. Uganda	4	3	12	—	1	7	1	—
77-1	US v. Nicaragua	4	3	12	—	1	2	1	—
78-1	US v. Libya	2	2	4	J	1	5+	3	—
81-1	US v. Nicaragua	2	2	4	Q	1	2+	2	—
82-3	Netherlands v. Suriname	2	3	6	—	2	1+	1	—

Notes: See table 3.5.

TABLE 3.3   Disruption of military adventures (other than major wars): political variables

Case[a]	Sender and target	Policy result[b] (index)	Sanctions contribution[c] (index)	Success score[d] (index)	Companion policies[e]	International cooperation[f] (index)	Sanctions period[g] (years)	Health and stability[h] (index)	Other goals[i]
21-1	League v. Yugoslavia	4	4	16	—	3	1	2	—
25-1	League v. Greece	4	4	16	—	3	1	2	—
32-1	League v. Paraguay/ Bolivia	3	2	6	—	3	3	2	—
35-1	League v. Italy	1	1	1	—	4	1	3	—
40-1	US v. Japan	1	1	1	—	3	1	3	—
48-1	US v. Netherlands	4	4	16	—	1	1	2	—
49-2	US/CHINCOM v. China	1	1	1	R,Q	3	4*	3	D
56-3	US v. UK/France	4	3	12	—	1	1	2	—
60-3	US v. Cuba	1	1	1	Q,J	3	23+	3	B
63-1	US v. UAR	4	4	16	—	1	2	2	A
63-3	US v. Indonesia	4	2	8	J	1	3	2	B
71-1	US v. India/Pakistan	2	1	2	Q	1	1	2	—
74-1	US v. Turkey	1	1	1	—	1	4	2	—
80-1	US v. USSR (Afghan)	1	1	1	Q	3	1	3	D
82-1	UK v. Argentina	4	3	12	R	2	1	2	—

*For this category, the length of the episode extends through the Korean War period.
Notes: See table 3.5.

TABLE 3.4 Impairment of military potential (including major wars): political variables

Case[a]	Sender and target	Policy result[b] (index)	Sanctions contri- bution[c] (index)	Success score[d] (index)	Companion policies[e]	International cooperation[f] (index)	Sanctions period[g] (years)	Health and stability[h] (index)	Other goals[i]
14-1	UK v. Germany	4	3	12	R	4	4	3	—
39-1	Western Allies v. Germany & Japan	4	3	12	R	4	6	3	—
46-1	Arab League v. Israel	2	2	4	R	3	37+	3	—
48-5	US/COCOM V. USSR/ COMECON	2	2	4	—	4	35+	3	C
49-2	US/CHINCOM v. China	1	1	1	R,Q	3	21	3	C
60-2	USSR v. China	2	2	4	Q	3	10	3	—
80-1	US v. USSR (Afghan)	1	1	1	Q	3	1	3	C
81-4	US v. USSR (Poland)	1	1	1	—	2	1	3	—

Notes: See table 3.5.

TABLE 3.5 Other major changes in target country policies (including surrender of territory): political variables

Case[a]	Sender and target	Policy result[b] (index)	Sanctions contri- bution[c] (index)	Success score[d] (index)	Companion policies[e]	International cooperation[f] (index)	Sanctions period[g] (years)	Health and stability[h] (index)	Other goals[i]
17-1	US v. Japan	2	2	4	—	1	1	3	—
48-3	USSR v. US/UK/France	1	1	1	Q	1	1	3	—
54-3	Spain v. UK	1	1	1	Q	1	29+	3	—
56-1	US v. Israel	2	1	2	—	1	4	3	—
57-1	Indonesia v. Netherlands	4	2	8	Q,R	2	5	3	—

(continued overleaf)

TABLE 3.5   Other major changes in target country policies (including surrender of territory): political variables (*continued*)

Case[a]	Sender and target	Policy result[b] (index)	Sanctions contribution[c] (index)	Success score[d] (index)	Companion policies[e]	International cooperation[f] (index)	Sanctions period[g] (years)	Health and stability[h] (index)	Other goals[i]
61-3	Western Allies v.								
	East Germany	1	1	1	—	3	1	3	—
62-2	UN v. South Africa	1	1	1	—	3	21+	3	—
63-2	Indonesia v. Malaysia	1	1	1	R	1	4	2	—
65-4	US v. Arab League	2	3	6	—	1	18+	3	—
73-1	Arab League v.								
	US/Netherlands	3	3	9	—	3	1	3	—
81-3	US v. Poland	2	2	4	—	3	2+	1	—

Notes, tables 3.1 through 3.5: The information in these tables is preliminary and subject to revision.

a. The *case* refers to the identification system used in table 1.1.

b. The *policy result*, on an index scale of 1 to 4, indicates the extent to which the outcome sought by the sender country was achieved. Key: (1) failed outcome; (2) unclear but possibly positive; (3) positive outcome; (4) successful outcome.

c. The *sanctions contribution*, on an index scale of 1 to 4, indicates the extent to which the sanctions contributed to a positive policy result. Key: (1) zero or negative contribution; (2) minor contribution; (3) modest contribution; (4) significant contribution.

d. The *success score* is an index on a scale of 1 to 16, found by multiplying the index of policy result by the index of sanctions contribution.

e. *Companion policies* refer to covert action (J), quasi-military operations (Q), and regular military action (R).

f. The extent of *international cooperation*, on an index scale of 1 to 4, indicates the degree of assistance received by the principal sender country in applying sanctions. Key: (1) no cooperation; (2) minor cooperation; (3) modest cooperation; (4) significant cooperation.

g. The *sanctions period* represents the rounded number of years, from first official threat or event to conclusion. The minimum period is one year. A (+) indicates that the sanction is still in effect.

h. *Health and stability* is an index, scaled from 1 to 3, that represents the target country's overall economic health and political stability (abstracting from sanctions) during the sanctions episode. Key: (1) distressed country; (2) country with significant problems; (3) strong and stable country.

i. *Other goals* refers to other sender objectives (these cases are listed under both headings). Key: (A) modest changes in target country policies; (B) destabilize the target government; (C) disrupt a military adventure (other than major wars); (D) impair the military potential of the target country (including sanctions imposed in major wars); (E) other major changes in target country policies (including territorial acquisition by the sender country).

4 Economic Variables

The economic variables in a sanctions episode are summarized in tables 4.1 through 4.5 (the tables appear at the end of this chapter). As in chapter 3, we have grouped the cases according to the major foreign policy objective. However, in this chapter we organize the discussion according to economic variables.

Size of Sender and Target Countries

The economy of the sender country is usually very much larger than the economy of the target country. In most cases, the sender's GNP is over 10 times greater than the target's GNP, and in almost half the cases the ratio is over 50. Indeed, the GNP ratio exceeds 100 in over 70 percent of the destabilization cases. These figures reflect, on the one hand, the prominence of the United States, the United Kingdom, and the USSR as senders, and, on the other hand, the small size of the countries they usually try to influence with economic sanctions.

In many instances, when the GNP ratio is under 10, sanctions flounder. Cases that entail major policy changes often belong to this category of failures. These cases either involve big power confrontations, or sender countries that are not major powers. Examples are the two world wars, the series of US-USSR confrontations, and Canadian attempts to advance nuclear nonproliferation policies in the mid-1970s. In several instances, however, sanctions were successful even though the GNP ratio was less than 10: the two world wars; US efforts against the United Kingdom and France during the Suez crisis of 1956; the Arab oil embargo against the United States and the Netherlands in 1973–74 (in this case, the GNP ratio was less than one); and the British sanctions during the Falklands war of 1982. But in most of these instances military victory was critical to the success of the episode.

These latter cases may explain why the GNP ratio is the only variable we tested through multiple regression analysis that was not consistent with our conclusions. A higher GNP ratio was associated with a lower success index. We attribute this surprising result to two phenomena: the close correlation between the GNP ratio and the type of policy goal, as noted above, and the correlation between the GNP ratio and the costs imposed on the target country, expressed as a percentage of GNP, discussed below. When we ran a correlation between the GNP ratio and the success score, without reference to the type of policy goal or other variables, the results confirmed our view that sanctions used by large countries against much smaller countries more often succeed. The statistical analysis will be discussed in greater detail in our forthcoming book.

Trade Linkages

Since sender countries are generally very large countries, it is not surprising that the target's import and export trade with the sender usually accounts for over 10 percent of the target's total trade. In the cases we have scored as successes, the sender country accounts, on average, for about a quarter of the target country's total trade. Even when the sender country interrupts only a small portion of that trade, the interruption carries an important message to the target country: change your policies or risk a larger disturbance.

The trade ratios in cases involving modest policy goals vary greatly. Some cases were successful when only a small amount of bilateral trade was involved (for example, *United States v. Ceylon*, 1961–65—9 percent of exports; 3 percent of imports). Many cases were unsuccessful even when a high proportion of trade was at stake, such as in the human rights episode of *United States v. Guatemala*, 1977–82, where over one-third of Guatemala's total trade was with the United States. In general, however, higher trade linkages are associated with success episodes (average trade linkage of 21 percent) than with failure episodes (average trade linkage of 15 percent).

Due to the usual close proximity of senders and targets in destabilization cases, their trade linkages are generally strong. One exception is the case *United Kingdom and United States v. Uganda*, 1972–79, over the misdeeds of the Idi Amin regime. But in almost every case in this group, the sender takes more than 10 percent of the exports, and supplies over 10 percent of the imports, of the target country. Within this group, the extent of linkage appears somewhat greater for success cases (average 34 percent) than for failure cases (average 27 percent).

Trade linkage does not appear to play a major role in episodes involving the disruption of military adventure, impairment of military potential, and other major policy changes, listed in tables 4.3, 4.4, and 4.5. Some successful cases involve high trade dependencies (*League v. Greece*, 1925; *United States v. United Arab Republic* 1963–65), while other successes occur when the bilateral trade relations are small (*United Kingdom v. Argentina*, 1982; in this case, however, the financial ties between the United Kingdom and

Argentina were much stronger than the trade ties). Conversely, high levels of bilateral trade do not ensure success, as is evident in the UN sanctions against South Africa from 1962 on, and Soviet measures against China in the 1960s.

Type of Sanction

Success may depend, to some extent, on whether the sanctions hit a sensitive sector in the target country's economy. A $100 million cost may have quite different effects—at home and abroad—depending on whether it is imposed by way of trade sanctions or by way of financial sanctions. Officials in the US State Department and other foreign ministries spend long hours tailoring their creations because they believe that the cut of a sanction matters a great deal.

The success of the Iranian asset freeze and the aid-denial cases of the 1960s involving Egypt, Brazil, India, and other countries, suggest that financial sanctions are generally more effective than trade sanctions. Why? In the first place, if the financial sanctions entail a reduction in official aid or credits they are not likely to create the same backlash, from business firms at home and allies abroad, as the interruption of private trade. In the second place, private financiers who might provide an alternative source of credit must anticipate a long-term relationship with the target country, and long-term relations are unsettled when financial sanctions are in the air.[1] In the third place, the denial of finance can disrupt the well-laid plans of powerful government ministers. By contrast, pain resulting from the shortage of goods can often (but not always) be spread across the populace at large.

An analysis of tables 4.1 through 4.5 indicates that financial leverage was deployed in 76 percent of the success cases; by comparison, export and import controls were each imposed in 42 percent of these cases. Of course many episodes involve the use of more than one type of sanction. Thus, financial sanctions played a role in almost two-thirds of the episodes, but the statistics indicate that they were more prominent in success cases than in failure cases.

When trade weapons are deployed, sender countries more frequently use

---

1. It should be noted that major capital projects, such as electric power plants, also involve long-term relations between countries.

export controls than import controls. One reason is that sender countries usually enjoy a more dominant market position as suppliers of exports than as purchasers of imports. Hence, for a given interruption of trade, sender countries can usually inflict greater pain by stopping exports than by stopping imports. The dominant position of the United States as a manufacturer of military hardware and high technology equipment has particularly influenced the tactics of US involvement with economic sanctions. A second reason for the emphasis on export controls, peculiar to the United States, is that the Congress has given the president much greater flexibility to restrain exports than to slow imports. Exports may be stopped readily through the mechanisms of the Export Administration Act, whereas imports can be slowed only by invoking the more cumbersome International Emergency Economic Powers Act, the national security section (section 232) of the Trade Expansion Act of 1962, or pre-existing quota legislation (such as sugar or textile quotas).

Our analysis does not indicate whether export or import controls are more frequently associated with success episodes. Indeed, there are so few cases of import controls imposed in isolation that it might be impossible to reach an informed judgment on this question. However, it is worth pointing out that export controls often result in a concentrated burden on individual companies in the sender country, whereas import controls usually spread the burden more widely. This is at least a reason for devising statutes that make it equally easy (or equally hard) for the executive branch to impose import controls as export controls.[2]

The Cost of Sanctions

Sanctions are supposed to impose economic penalties in order to coerce the target country to alter its policies; if the sanctions impose no costs, they are unlikely to change foreign behavior. In short, according to the underlying rationale, the level of costs importantly determines the success or failure of a sanctions episode.

---

2. GATT Article XXI enables a country to take "any action which it considers necessary for its national security interests. . ." It remains to be determined whether import and export controls imposed for foreign policy purposes fall within the purview of this provision, and whether a distinction would be made between controls on imports of sugar and controls on exports of pipelaying equipment. Part of the answer may come in the current Nicaraguan-GATT case challenging US sanctions on sugar imports from Nicaragua.

COSTS TO TARGETS

Some economists have constructed fairly elaborate theoretical models to suggest how the conditions of supply and demand for the sanctioned commodity might affect the level of costs incurred by the sender and imposed on the target, and how the balance of costs might affect the outcome of a sanctions episode. Unfortunately, the more elaborate the model the less likely that it is tarnished by economic data. In fact, few studies go beyond anecdotal accounts of the costs that economic sanctions impose on target countries. We have, therefore, developed a very simple analytical construct to guide our own rudimentary efforts to estimate the costs imposed on the target country. Our methodology is detailed in appendix B.

In order to calculate the cost of each sanctions episode to the target country, we have estimated the initial deprivation of markets, supplies, or finance, expressed on an annualized basis in current US dollars. To calculate the "welfare loss" to the target's economy, we then used our own judgment to estimate the "sanctions multiplier" that should be applied in the context of the particular episode. Some types of sanctions affect the target country more than others for a given amount of trade or finance. The welfare loss caused by reductions in aid may be 100 percent of the value of the aid; on the other hand, trade controls may cause less harm than the value of the shipments affected because of the availability of other markets or substitution for other goods.

We recognize that the third law of physics—for every action there is a reaction—seems to play a role in the course of a sanctions episode. The impact of sanctions on the target country may be partially or totally offset by the helping hand of another major power. There are several instances where the target has actually become better off, in economic terms, as a result of the sanctions. Soviet attempts to pressure Yugoslavia in 1948 failed miserably from Moscow's perspective, but yielded Tito an abundant harvest of Western aid and trade credits. In a similar fashion, American efforts to coerce Ethiopia on human rights and compensation issues helped push Colonel Mengistu into the waiting and generous arms of the Russians. In our cost estimates, we attempt to reflect these offsetting benefits.

A brief survey of three cases may help illustrate our calculations of economic costs.

League of Nations v. Italy (1935–36: Ethiopia)

In a belated attempt to coerce Italy into withdrawing its troops from Ethiopia, the League agreed in late 1935 to a limited trade embargo and to restrictions on loans and credits to Italy. The sanctions did not include key commodities such as oil, nor were they applied by some League and non-League members (for example, the United States). Nonetheless, trade was sharply reduced from the presanction period. Financial conditions in Italy were also affected by the sanctions (and the cost of the war): the lira was devalued by 25 percent in November 1935, and Italy was forced to sell about $94 million in gold between November 1935 and June 1936 to bolster its dwindling reserves.

The sanctions caused a decline in both exports and imports, and a forced sale of gold reserves. During the six months when sanctions were in effect, exports dropped by $56 million and imports by $72 million from the previous year's levels. Yet, in analyzing this period, M. J. Bonn noted that "[s]tocks on hand, the practice of economies, the development of substitutes, and the purchase of goods with gold, foreign securities, emigrants' remittances and tourists' disbursements kept the country going without too severe a strain."[3] The "elasticity of substitution" was undoubtedly high. Accordingly, we estimated the welfare loss to the Italian economy at 30 percent of the value of interrupted trade, or $34 million and $43 million, respectively, for exports and imports, when calculated on an annualized basis. In addition, we estimated that Italy incurred a financial loss of $9 million because of forced gold sales, which we estimated to have been made at a 10 percent discount. In sum, we estimate that the sanctions led to an $86 million loss in welfare to the Italian economy, equal to 1.7 percent of GNP.

USSR v. Yugoslavia (1948–55: Nationalism)

Stalin used economic pressure and threats of military intervention in an attempt to force Tito back into the Soviet fold. Almost all economic ties between Yugoslavia and the Soviet bloc were suspended by mid-1949. The sanctions led Yugoslavia to expand its trade and to seek military and economic aid from the West. Total trade flows were not reduced but there was a dramatic shift in the direction of trade: in 1948, over 50 percent of Yugoslav trade was with the Soviet Union and Eastern Europe; by 1954, over 80 percent of trade was with the United States and Western Europe.

Yugoslavia claimed it lost $400 million between 1948 and 1954 as a result

---

3. See M. J. Bonn, "How Sanctions Failed," 15 *Foreign Affairs* (January 1937), p. 360.

of the Soviet sanctions. Our calculations are in the same ball park. We took the amount of credits offered to Yugoslavia at the end of the sanctions episode as a surrogate for the reduction in aid from the COMECON countries. The Soviet bloc offered $289 million in credits in 1955. Spreading the credits over a six-year period and estimating the welfare loss at 75 percent of the value of the aid yields an annualized cost of $36 million. The suspension of payments on COMECON debts also cost the Yugoslavs about $300 million over the period 1948–54, which when valued at 70 percent of the lost revenues, led to a further loss of $35 million per year. The confrontation with the Soviet bloc also caused a sharp increase in military expenditures, which accounted for 22 percent of national income during 1950–54.[4] The increase in the military budget was directly attributable to the heightened tensions caused by the Soviet sanctions; accordingly, we also took account of increases in the Yugoslav military budget over the sanctions period. Annual military expenditures in 1950–54 ran about $162 million above the 1948 level; we estimated the annual welfare loss at 25 percent of the additional expenditures, or $40.5 million a year.

These various costs amounted to 3.6 percent of Yugoslav GNP in 1952. However, the costs were more than offset by compensating aid flows from the United States and Europe, and loans from the World Bank. From 1950–54, Yugoslavia received about $1 billion in military and economic aid from the West. Clearly, such funds would not have been forthcoming in the absence of a breach in the Soviet bloc. We estimated Yugoslavia's welfare gain as 75 percent of the transfers, or $187.5 million a year. As a result, there was an annual net welfare *gain* to the Yugoslav economy during this period of $76 million, equal to 2.5 percent of GNP.

United States v. Dominican Republic, (1960–62: Trujillo)

The notorious abuses of Rafael Trujillo prompted the United States, in 1960, to impose a limited trade embargo to destabilize the Trujillo regime. The embargo covered arms, petroleum products, trucks and spare parts. In addition the United States imposed a special two cents a pound entry fee for nonquota sugar imported from the Dominican Republic. While multilateral in nature,

---

4. See R. Barry Farrell, *Yugoslavia and the Soviet Union 1948–1956* (Hamden, Connecticut: Shoe String Press, 1956), pp. 27–30.

for all practical purposes the sanctions were imposed only by the United States.

The most costly measure was the US sugar fee. It has been estimated elsewhere[5] that this fee cost the Dominican Republic about $12.5 million per year. Imports of the sanctioned petroleum products fell by 25 percent, but limited product coverage and alternate sourcing in Europe softened the impact on the Dominican economy. Accordingly, we estimated the annual welfare loss at 30 percent of the trade affected by the sanctions, or only $0.7 million on an annual basis. Imports of trucks, buses, and parts were so small that the losses caused by the sanctions had a negligible impact. Nonetheless, in the aggregate the sanctions put the squeeze on an already shaky economy, and contributed both to a drop in per capita GNP from $293 in 1960 to $267 in 1961 and to a decline of $28 million in gold and foreign exchange reserves. We estimated that the drop in reserves resulted in a welfare loss of $2.8 million (based on 10 percent of the decline). Overall, the sanctions cost the Dominican Republic some $16 million, equal to 1.9 percent of GNP in 1960.

As these three examples show, we tried to err on the side of overestimating the economic impact of sanctions on target countries. Nevertheless, we uncovered few cases where sanctions inflicted a heavy cost relative to national income. Very seldom did the costs of sanctions (expressed on an annualized basis) reach even 1 percent of the target country's GNP. Of course, government officials fight very hard for policy changes that might change GNP by 1 percent; and elections are won or lost, and coups are staged, with the expenditure of far less money. Still, the numbers seem small.

Why don't sanctions impose a heavier cost on the target country? The most important reason is that sender countries encounter great difficulty in extending the net of sanctions to cover a broad range of economic activity and a large number of trading partners. Even when allied governments embark on a joint sanctions effort, the obstacles are formidable. Sanctions create powerful incentives for evasion. Indeed, it could be said that a sieve leaks like a sanction. Ingenious new trading relationships, devised by domestic and third-country firms, flower because it is difficult to trace the origin and destination of traded goods. In the 1980s, Iran and Argentina obtained spare military parts, and Libya marketed its oil in Europe—albeit at some cost and delay—thanks to triangular trade arrangements. Moreover, transshipments can be routed through friendly (or at least not antagonistic) countries: for

---

5. See C. Lloyd Brown-John, *Multilateral Sanctions*, p. 229.

many years, the lifeline for Rhodesia was its continuing trade with South Africa, Zambia, and Mozambique.

Despite these many leakages, sanctions do impose a cost. And when the costs of the sanctions are over 1 percent of GNP, sanctions usually succeed. Destabilization episodes stand out as cases where the sender country is generally willing and able to turn the screws hard. In over 75 percent of the destabilization cases, the cost of sanctions equaled or exceeded 1 percent of GNP. By contrast, when a sender seeks modest policy goals, it seldom inflicts heavy costs—in fewer than 15 percent of the cases listed in table 4.1 did the costs exceed 1 percent of GNP. Yet even sanctions that exert a modest impact relative to GNP can contribute to the successful achievement of foreign policy goals. The fear of deprivation can be just as important as deprivation itself. Moreover, policy decisions often turn on amounts that are quite small in GNP terms.

COSTS TO SENDERS

Foreign policy measures generally entail domestic costs, and sanctions episodes are no exception. Domestic firms pay an immediate price when trade, aid, or financial flows are disrupted. Moreover, sanctions increase the long-term uncertainty, and therefore the cost, of doing business abroad. All trading partners of the sender country, not just the target country, may be prompted to seek diversified sources of supply, alternative partners for joint ventures, and technologies not developed in the sender country.

There is a limited exception to the general rule that sanctions entail costs for the sender country. If the sender seeks to coerce the target by cutting aid or official credits, the sender may enjoy an immediate economic gain due to a reduction in budget expenditures. But even in these instances, the corollary loss of trade contacts may entail an economic burden—in the form of lost sales and jobs—on the sender country.

It is often said that the sender country in a sanctions episode should seek to maximize its political gains and to minimize its economic costs. Sometimes this advice is translated into the recommendation that the sender country should seek to maximize the ratio of costs inflicted to costs incurred. At best, these precepts are honored in the abstract. The domestic costs of a sanctions episode are rarely calculated—and almost never in advance—for two basic reasons.

First of all, it is just plain hard to quantify the costs to the sender country.

Too many intangible factors are at play. If the green eyeshade staff of the Office of Management and Budget were ever asked to calculate the costs of imposing sanctions, they would be aghast. Hard data rarely exist. And many costs will only appear years later as a result of lost sales opportunities and deferred investment plans which befall firms branded with the tag of "unreliable supplier."

The second reason for not making advance calculations is that, for large countries, the overall impact on the sender's economy may be regarded as trivial. In most of the cases we have examined, the cost to the target is less than 1 percent of its GNP. The costs borne by sender countries, as a percent of their GNP levels, usually will be very much less, since they have much larger economies. From the lofty perspective of the White House or 10 Downing Street, the costs may seem entirely affordable.

However, the recent US grain embargo and pipeline sanctions focused attention on the very different perspective of individual firms. Sanctions are paid for by the industries whose trade is most deeply affected. By contrast, most other foreign and defense policies are financed out of general treasury revenues. Under present procedures, sanctions amount to a discriminatory, sector-specific tax to finance foreign policy—an approach that seems entirely unfair.

It may be useful to illustrate our construction of the cost-to-sender index through a review of two cases.

United States v. South Korea (1973–77: Human Rights)

Sanctions generally impose small costs on domestic economic interests—and generate little or no domestic political opposition—when they involve the closing of the bilateral aid spigot. This is clearly illustrated by US actions in support of improved human rights in South Korea following President Park's declaration of martial law in 1972. The average US citizen did not feel the pinch from the substantial cutback in economic aid (mostly PL-480 food aid) and military aid to South Korea; indeed, the US budget "profited" from the reduced expenditures, although the reduction of a few hundred million dollars in aid transfers had little impact on the US budget deficits that were run up during this period.

From 1974–78, average US economic and military aid to South Korea declined by over $450 million from the average level of the period 1970–73. While the cutbacks in PL-480 and military aid led to some increased costs for the United States (for example, in storage and other incidental expenses for grain), the short-run impact on the US budget was minimal (about 1 percent of the deficit) but favorable. In this case, the cost to the sender was negative—the United States was actually slightly better off, in economic terms, as a result of the sanctions. This result illustrates those cases that we accorded a cost-to-sender index number of 1.

United States v. USSR (1980–   : Afghanistan)

Much has been written about the economic impact of the grain embargo on the US farm sector. When the Carter administration imposed the embargo in January 1980, it estimated that US farm income would be reduced by $2.0 billion to $2.25 billion as a result of a cut of 17 million tons in grain shipped to the Soviet Union. Corresponding measures were introduced to soften the blow on the US farmer, entailing purchases for the grain reserve and increases in loan, release, and call prices. These measures added an additional $2 billion to $3 billion to the federal deficit during FY 1980 and 1981.[6] The purchases for the grain reserve, which sopped up about $2.4 billion in grain that would have been dumped on the market after the embargo was announced, ended up costing the US taxpayer (according to estimates of the General Accounting Office) over $600 million in direct budgetary expenditures, including costs incurred in the purchase, storage, and resale of the grain.

The extent to which the embargo imposed a welfare loss on the US farm sector as a whole is more problematical. The Congressional Research Service noted that it took nine months for wheat, corn, and soybean prices to recover from the shock of the onset of the embargo[7]; at the same time, farm income plummeted, although how much of the fall was due to the embargo and how much to other factors (for example, high interest rates) is hard to quantify. In any event, US farmers lost a significant share of the Soviet market. Even though the US share of the world market actually grew by 2 percent in the

---

6. *Weekly Compilation of Presidential Documents,* 28 January 1980, pp. 105 ff.

7. Congressional Research Service, *An Assessment of the Afghanistan Sanctions: Implications for Trade and Diplomacy in the 1980s* (Washington: US Government Printing Office, 1981), pp. 45–46.

1980–81 marketing year compared to pre-embargo levels,[8] these lost sales to the USSR probably imposed a welfare loss to US farmers through their effect on prices and stunted trade opportunities.

The grain embargo was accompanied by export controls on high technology products and superphosphoric acid, affecting close to $500 million in prospective US exports. Using the same methodology that we employed to calculate the cost to the target country, we would estimate the welfare loss to US producers, after account is made for substitution and price effects, as about 30 percent of the value of trade affected by the sanctions. This translates into $150 million for superphosphoric acid and high technology products and at least $600 million for farm goods. In sum, the sanctions against the USSR—while difficult to quantify—did inflict significant costs on US economic interests. In GNP terms, the costs to the United States were negligible; yet the sanctions did result in substantial trade diversion—and important losses for specific sectors of the US economy. These loans in turn created "political" problems for the administration. We have not based our cost-to-sender index on costs as a percentage of GNP; instead we only consider whether there has been a modest or substantial level of trade diversion which might be expected to create, as it did in this case, domestic political opposition to the sanctions. By this standard, the Afghanistan case was given an index of "3" to reflect the cost-to-sender.

In just under half the cases involving modest policy goals listed in table 4.1, the sender country enjoyed a net gain (usually quite small) as a result of withholding aid and official credits. The only episode in this group where significant trade diversion occurred, with consequent losses to the firms in the sender country, was the Iranian hostage case.

The successful destabilization cases listed in table 4.2, except for the Rhodesian sanctions episode, generally cost the sender country rather little. The average cost index number for the successful cases was 1.6. By contrast, the average for failed cases was 1.9, and some of the episodes were rather expensive to the sender. US traders have long since adjusted to the Cuban embargo, but the initial measures entailed losses of some consequence for particular US industries. In the Libyan case, some US oil companies were

---

8. Office of Technology Assessment, *Technology and East-West Trade: An Update* (Washington: US Government Printing Office, 1983), p. 54.

placed in a disadvantaged position. Exxon, for one, settled for a payment substantially less than book-value for its Libyan assets.

In the successful cases involving disruption of military adventures, listed in table 4.3, the average cost index to the sender was just 1.5. For disruption cases with failed outcomes, the cost index was 2.2. Here again, it is evident that failed episodes were generally more costly to the sender—a finding that will come as no surprise to the farmers affected by the Soviet grain embargo.

When countries resort to sanctions in order to impair the military potential of target countries, or to pursue other major policy changes, not only are they distinctly unsuccessful (short of all-out war) but they also invariably accept a significant economic burden. In the success cases, the costs to the sender were understandably great in the two world war cases, and the Arabs clearly gained from the oil embargo. However, this sample is too small to yield clear trends. The average cost-to-sender index in the failed, impaired military potential cases was 3.3; the average cost-to-sender index in the failed, other major policy change cases was 2.3. While small in GNP terms, the annualized cost figures probably run in the hundreds of millions of dollars and those losses are usually concentrated on relatively few firms.

To summarize: higher failure rates are associated with greater costs borne by the sender country. On the one hand, failed cases may entail intrinsically tougher objectives and the sender government may be willing to expend greater effort in achieving its goals; on the other hand, as costs mount, pressures may arise within the sender country to abandon the attempt, thereby contributing to the failure of the episode.

TABLE 4.1 Modest changes in target country policies: economic variables

Case[a]	Sender and target	Success score[b] (index)	Cost to target[c] (million dollars)	Cost as percentage of GNP[d]	Trade linkage[e] (percentage)	GNP ratio[f]: sender to target	Type of sanction[h]	Cost to sender[i] (index)
33-1	UK v. USSR	12	4	negl.	13	1	M	2
38-1	US/UK v. Mexico	9	2	0.1	70	75	F,M	2
54-1	USSR v. Australia	1	50	0.5	3	18	M	2
61-1	US v. Ceylon	16	5	0.4	6	374	F	1
63-1	US v. UAR	16	54	1.4	25	153	F	1
65-1	US v. Chile	12	0.5	negl.	37	90	F,M	2
65-2	US v. India	16	10	negl.	24	14	F	1
68-2	US v. Peru	16	35	0.7	10	185	F	1
73-2	US v. S. Korea	12	333	1.8	29	78	F	1
73-3	US v. Chile	9	35	0.4	18	187	F	1
74-2	Canada v. India	6	33	negl.	2	2	X	1
74-3	Canada v. Pakistan	4	13	negl.	2	14	X	2
75-1	US/Canada v. S. Korea	16	nil	nil	27	78	—	2
75-2	US v. USSR	4	57	negl.	6	2	M	2
75-3	US v. Eastern Europe	12	23	negl.	2	6	M	1
75-4	US v. S. Africa	4	2	negl.	12	43	X	2
76-1	US v. Uruguay	6	10	0.3	10	452	F	1
76-2	US v. Taiwan	16	17	0.1	32	100	X	2
76-3	US v. Ethiopia	1	(310)	(11.0)	22	592	F,M	1
77-1	US v. Paraguay	6	2	0.1	13	950	F	2
77-2	US v. Guatemala	4	19	0.3	37	352	F	1

TABLE 4.1   Modest changes in target country policies: economic variables (*continued*)

Case[a]	Sender and target	Success score[b] (index)	Cost to target[c] (million dollars)	Cost as percentage of GNP[d]	Trade linkage[e] (percentage)	GNP ratio[f]: sender to target	Type of sanction[h]	Cost to sender[i] (index)
77-3	US v. Argentina	6	62	0.1	13	38	F,X	2
77-4	Canada v. Japan	16	75	negl.	3	0.3	X	2
78-1	China v. Albania	1	43	3.3	50	249	F	1
78-2	US v. Brazil	6	5	negl.	22	11	X	2
78-3	US v. Argentina	6	negl.	negl.	14	34	X	2
78-4	US v. India	6	12	negl.	13	18	X	2
79-1	US v. Iran	12	3,349	4.0	11	28	F,X,M	3
79-2	US v. Pakistan	6	34	0.2	10	113	F,X	1
79-3	Arab League v. Canada	12	7	negl.	2	1	F,X,M	2
80-2	US v. Iraq	4	22	0.1	6	69	X	2

Notes: See table 4.5.

TABLE 4.2 **Destabilization of target governments: economic variables**

Case[a]	Sender and target	Success score[b] (index)	Cost to target[c] (million dollars)	Cost as percentage of GNP[d]	Trade linkage[e] (percentage)	GNP ratio[f]: sender to target	Type of sanction[h]	Cost to sender[i] (index)
18-1	UK v. Russia	1	446	4.1	18	1	F,X,M	3
44-1	US v. Argentina	4	29	0.8	19	58	F	1
48-4	USSR v. Yugoslavia	1	(76)	(2.5)	13	52	F,X,M	1
51-1	UK/US v. Iran	12	186	14.0	42	235	F,M	1
56-4	US v. Laos	9	5	4.2	2	4,375	F	1
58-1	USSR v. Finland	16	45	1.0	19	59	F,X,M	2
60-1	US v. Dominican Republic	16	16	2.0	56	596	F,X,M	2
60-3	US v. Cuba	1	114	4.0	46	140	F,X,M	3
61-2	USSR v. Albania	1	9	1.8	52	494	F,X,M	2
62-1	US v. Brazil	12	110	0.6	49	30	F	1
63-3	US v. Indonesia	8	110	2.0	25	145	F	1
65-3	UK/UN v. Rhodesia	12	123	12.0	69	1,388	F,X,M	3
70-2	US v. Chile	12	163	1.5	17	102	F	1
72-2	UK/US v. Uganda	12	32	2.3	22	860	F,X,M	2
77-1	US v. Nicaragua	12	12	0.6	26	913	F,X	1
78-8	US v. Libya	4	91	0.5	26	118	X,M	3
81-1	US v. Nicaragua	6	(47)	(3.4)	35	1,727	F,M	2
82-3	Netherlands v. Surinam	6	99	10.0	13	160	F	1

Notes: See table 4.5.

TABLE 4.3 Disruption of military adventures (other than major wars): economic variables

Case[a]	Sender and target	Success score[b] (index)	Cost to target[c] (million dollars)	Cost as percentage of GNP[d]	Trade linkage[e] (percentage)	GNP ratio[f]: sender to target	Type of sanction[h]	Cost to sender[i] (index)
21-1	League v. Yugoslavia	16	—	—	26	37	—	1
25-1	League v. Greece	16	—	—	36	56	X	2
32-1	League v. Paraguay/Bolivia	6	6	4.5	41	224	X	2
35-1	League v. Italy	1	86	1.7	16	6	F,X,M	3
40-1	US v. Japan	1	66	0.7	31	11	X	3
48-1	US v. Netherlands	16	14	0.2	9	45	F	1
49-2	US/CHINCOM v. China	1	106	0.5	38	13	F,X,M	3
56-3	US v. UK/France	12	28	negl.	9	4	F	2
60-3	US v. Cuba	1	114	4.0	46	140	F,X,M	3
63-1	US v. UAR	16	54	1.4	25	153	F	1
63-3	US v. Indonesia	8	110	2.0	25	145	F	1
71-1	US v. India/Pakistan	2	117	0.2	19	16	F,X	1
74-1	US v. Turkey	1	77	0.2	12	42	F	1
80-1	US v. USSR	1	525	negl.	4	2	X	3
82-1	UK v. Argentina	12	1,059	0.7	5	3	F,X,M	2

Notes: See table 4.5.

TABLE 4.4 Impairment of military potential (including major wars): economic variables

Case[a]	Sender and target	Success score[b] (index)	Cost to target[c] (million dollars)	Cost as percentage of GNP[d]	Trade linkage[e] (percentage)	GNP ratio[f]: sender to target	Type of sanction[h]	Cost to sender[i] (index)
14-1	UK v. Germany	12	843	7.0	9	1	F,X,M	4
39-1	Western Allies v. Germany/Japan	12	688	1.6	15	2	F,X,M	4
46-1	Arab League v. Israel	4	258	2.1	2	2	F,X,M	4
48-5	US/COCOM v. USSR/COMECON	4	270	0.1	32	5	X	3
49-2	US/CHINCOM v. China	1	106	0.5	38	13	F,X,M	3
60-2	USSR v. China	4	120	0.1	46	3	F,X,M	4
80-1	US v. USSR (Afghan)	1	525	negl.	4	2	X	3
81-3	US v. USSR (Poland)	1	355	negl.	4	2	X	3

Notes: See table 4.5.

TABLE 4.5 Other major changes in target country policies (including surrender of territory): economic variables

Case[a]	Sender and target	Success score[b] (index)	Cost to target[c] (million dollars)	Cost as percentage of GNP[d]	Trade linkage[e] (percentage)	GNP ratio[f]: sender to target	Type of sanction[h]	Cost to sender[i] (index)
17-1	US v. Japan	4	23	0.8	20	13	X	2
48-3	USSR v. US/UK/France	1	251	negl.	1	0.3	X,M	2
54-3	Spain v. UK	1	5	negl.	1	0.2	X,M	3
56-1	US v. Israel	2	16	0.1	20	134	F	2
57-1	Indonesia v. Netherlands	8	69	0.7	2	0.2	F,X,M	1
61-3	Western Allies v. East Germany	1	—	—	12	40	X,M	2
62-2	UN v. South Africa	1	273	1.0	77	130	F,X	3
63-2	Indonesia v. Malaysia	1	29	1.0	6	2	X,M	3
65-4	US v. Arab League	6	2	negl.	12	35	F,X	2
73-1	Arab League v. US/Netherlands	9	5,697	0.4	2	negl.	X	1
81-2	US v. Poland	4	62	negl.	4	16	F,X	3

Notes, tables 4.1 through 4.5: Nil indicates zero; negl. indicates very small. The information in these tables is preliminary and subject to revision.

a. The *case* refers to the identification system used in table 1.1.

b. The *success score* is an index on a scale of 1 to 16, found by multiplying the index of policy result by the index of sanctions contribution (see tables 3.1 through 3.5).

c. The *cost to target* is expressed in terms of millions of current US dollars, as estimated in the abstracts. Parentheses around a cost figure indicate a gain to the target country.

d. The *cost as percentage of GNP* refers to the cost of sanctions to the target country as a percentage of its GNP. Parentheses indicate a gain.

e. The *trade linkage* equals the average of presanction target country exports to the sender country (as a percentage of total target country exports) and imports from the sender country (as a percentage of total target country imports).

f. The *GNP ratio* refers to the ratio of the sender country GNP to the target country GNP.

h. The *type of sanction* refers to the interruption of commercial finance, aid and other official finance (F), the interruption of exports from the sender country to the target country (X), and the interruption of imports by the sender country from the target country (M).

i. The *cost to sender* is an index number scaled from 1 to 4. Key: (1) net gain to sender; (2) little effect on sender; (3) modest welfare loss to sender; (4) major loss to sender.

5   Conclusions

A number of lessons can be abstracted from the sanctions episodes of the past seventy years. In this concluding chapter, we first assess the overall effectiveness of sanctions, based on the 78 cases abstracted to date.[1] We then group the lessons learned into a list of propositions—nine commandments—to guide governments in deciding when sanctions might help achieve their foreign policy goals.

Are Sanctions Effective?

Policymakers need to take a close look at the cost and effectiveness of sanctions when setting out their foreign policy strategy. In many cases, sanctions do not contribute very much to the achievement of publicly stated foreign policy goals; however, in some instances sanctions have helped alter the policies of target countries. Table 5.1 summarizes the score card. By our standards, success cases are those with a success score of nine or higher; failure cases are those with a score of eight or lower.

TABLE 5.1   **Success by type of policy goal**

Policy goal	Success cases	Failure cases	Success ratio (percentage of total)
Modest policy changes	15	16	48
Destabilization	9	9	50
Disruption of military adventures	6	9	40
Military impairment	2	6	25
Other major policy changes	1	10	9
Totals[a]	33	50	40

a. The figures include five instances of cases included under two different policy goals: 49-2: US v. China; 60-3: US v. Cuba; 63-1: US vs. UAR; 63-3: US v. Indonesia; and 80-1: US v. USSR (Afghanistan). Since these cases are generally failures, double-counting them adds a small negative bias to the success ratio.

---

1. Recall that cases between second- and third-ranking powers are probably underrepresented in our abstracts, because some of them have been inadvertently omitted from the universe of cases listed in table 1.1 and because we concentrated, in the first instance, on abstracting the major cases.

Perhaps surprisingly, sanctions have been successful in 40 percent of the cases. The success rate importantly depends on type of goal, however. Episodes involving destabilization succeed in half the cases, disruption of military adventures and modest goals are attained in almost half the cases (although the success rate for modest goal cases has recently dropped; see below), but attempts to impair a foreign adversary's military potential, or otherwise change its policies in a major way, generally fail.

Success has proven much more elusive in recent years than in earlier decades. This point is made in table 5.2. Taking the pre-1973 period as a whole, almost half (45 percent) of the episodes succeeded. In the decade 1973–83, the success rate was less than a third. The difference seems to reflect an abundance of episodes seeking modest policy changes, with less than fruitful outcomes. Before 1973, these cases accounted for only 16 percent of episodes we have documented; since then, modest goals have inspired the use of sanctions in 68 percent of the cases. The success rate in these cases dropped markedly between the two periods, from 87 percent to 35 percent.

TABLE 5.2   **Success by period**

	Pre-1973		1973–83	
Policy goal	Success cases	Failure cases	Success cases	Failure cases
Modest policy changes	7	1	8	15
Destabilization	8	6	1	3
Disruption of military adventures	5	7	1	2
Military impairment	2	4	0	2
Other major policy changes	0	9	1	1
Totals	22	27	11	23

Quite conceivably, with the frequent use of economic sanctions to achieve modest goals, target countries have become more immune to their impact. This immunity may derive from two factors: first, latter-day target countries are less dependent on trade with sender countries; and second, more nations are willing and able to play Sir Galahad to target countries. Ties between target and sender countries have become weaker: the trade linkage fell from 23 percent to 15 percent in recent cases compared to the pre-1973 period. Many of the failures in recent years are connected with the widespread use of sanctions by the United States in support of human rights and nuclear nonproliferation campaigns against countries as remote as Pakistan and Argentina. Moreover, the growth in global economic interdependence and the East-West confrontation have made it easier for target countries to find alternate suppliers, markets, and financial backers, to replace goods embargoed or funds withheld by the sender country.

Nine Commandments

From the summary in table 5.1, it is clear that sanctions can bear fruit when planted in the right soil and nurtured in the proper way. Nine propositions are offered for the statesman who would act as a careful gardener.

I.   "DON'T BITE OFF MORE THAN YOU CAN CHEW."

Sanctions cannot move mountains nor can they force strong target countries into making fundamental changes. Countries often have inflated expectations of what sanctions can and cannot accomplish. At most, there is a weak correlation between economic deprivation and political willingness to change. The *economic* impact of sanctions may be pronounced, both on the sender and the target country, but other factors in the situational context almost always overshadow the impact of sanctions in determining the *political* outcome.

Sanctions are seldom effective in impairing the military potential of an important power, or in bringing major changes in domestic policies of the target country. In cases involving these "high" policy goals,[2] success was achieved in only 3 of the 19 cases, or only 16 percent of the time. Excluding the two world wars, we have found only one case (*Arab League v. United States/Netherlands*)where economic coercion was effective in changing major domestic policies. In this case, the Arab oil embargo helped accomplish two of its four objectives: it caused a significant shift, namely a more pro-Arab slant, in European and Japanese policies toward the Palestinian question; and it supported OPEC's decision to boost the world price of oil to OPEC's enormous economic benefit; but the embargo failed to get Israel to retreat

---

2. We use the term "high" policy goals to refer only to military impairment and major policy change episodes. Some authors have used the same phrase to refer to destabilization and disruption of military adventure cases as well.

behind its pre-1967 frontiers, and it failed to cause the United States to abandon its pro-Israel policy stance. The sanctions were an important factor in the attainment of results that, on balance, must be deemed at least marginally successful from the Arab viewpoint. In the other cases where impairment was sought and attempts were made to change major policies of target countries—ranging from the lifting of martial law in Poland or to the ending of apartheid in South Africa—sanctions were ineffective.

To justify even a remote hope for success in military impairment and major change cases, sender countries would have to form a near monopoly over trading relations with the target country. This obvious precept, learned in World Wars I and II, was forgotten in the case of UN sanctions against South Africa and turned on its head in the recent case of US sanctions to block construction of the Soviet-European gas pipeline.

II. "BIG FISH EAT LITTLE FISH."

In the great majority of cases we have documented, the target country has been much smaller than the sender country. Thus, while sanctions typically involve only a small proportion of the trade or financial flows of the sender country, they can significantly affect the external accounts of the target country. The importance of size is illustrated by table 5.3. In cases involving modest goals, destabilization and disruption of military adventures, the sender's economy is generally over 50 times greater than the target's economy.

TABLE 5.3 **Success, size and trade linkage**

Policy goal	Average GNP ratio: sender to target		Average trade linkage	
	Success cases	Failure cases	Success cases (percentage)	Failure cases (percentage)
Modest goals	91	185	21	15
Destabilization	951	322	34	27
Disruption of military adventures	50	67	18	26
Military impairment	2	5	12	21
Other major policy changes	negl.	37	2	15
Totals	302	137	23	20

Indeed, the size differential is so great in these episodes that the difference in GNP ratios between success and failed cases does not seem to be significant.

For the "high" policy military impairment and major policy change cases, the figures in table 5.3 indicate that there is less of a size differential between sender and target. These episodes usually involve either big power confrontations or small power neighborhood fights.

The trade linkage data broadly confirm these propositions. Recall that trade linkage is measured as the average of the target country's imports from the sender as a percentage of its total imports and the target country's exports to the sender as a percentage of its total exports. In most episodes involving modest goals or destabilization attempts, the trade dependence exceeds 20 percent, and the trade linkage in success cases is generally higher than in failure cases. Cases involving disruption of military adventures also have trade linkages at the 20 percent level; in this category, failed cases exhibit a slightly higher trade linkage than successes. In the "high" policy cases (the last two categories), the trade linkage is usually less than 20 percent and the trade linkage is perversely higher in failed cases. Taking all categories together, successful cases exhibit a slightly higher trade linkage (23 percent) than failures (20 percent).

III.   "THE WEAKEST GO TO THE WALL."

Summing up all cases in the five groups, there seems to be a direct correlation between the political and economic health of the target country and its susceptibility to economic pressure. The only time that sanctions were successful against a country that we labeled "strong and stable" was in the mid-1970s, when South Korea twice yielded to US sanctions in deference to an overriding interest in the US-Korean bilateral security relationship. By contrast, countries in distress or experiencing significant problems are far more likely to succumb to the policy objectives of the sender country.

Table 5.4 clearly demonstrates this point. When specific goals are at issue, the health and stability of the target country is usually an important determinant in the success of the episode. This feature is most pronounced in destabilization cases, where successes came against generally weak regimes. The health and stability index was also significantly lower in success cases than in failure cases when disruption of military adventures were at stake. In cases involving modest policy goals, the health and stability of the target country seem to be less of a factor in determining success. In the "high" policy categories, there are too few success stories to yield a meaningful comparison.

TABLE 5.4 **Success, health and stability**

Policy goal	Average health and stability index	
	Success cases	Failure cases
Modest policy changes	2.2	2.4
Destabilization	1.4	2.1
Disruption of military adventures	2.0	2.6
Military impairment	3.0	3.0
Other major policy changes	3.0	2.7
Totals	2.0	2.5

IV. "IF IT WERE DONE WHEN 'TIS DONE, THEN 'TWERE WELL IT WERE DONE QUICKLY. . . ."

A heavy, slow hand invites both evasion and the mobilization of domestic opinion in the target country. Sanctions imposed slowly or incrementally may simply strengthen the target government at home as it mobilizes the forces of nationalism. Moreover, such measures are likely to be undercut over time either by the sender's own firms or by foreign competitors. Sanctions generally are regarded as a short-term policy, with the anticipation that normal commercial relations will be reestablished after the resolution of the crisis. This explains why, even though the public in the sender country often welcomes the introduction of sanctions, public support for sanctions dissipates over time.

TABLE 5.5 **Success and length of sanctions**

Policy goal	Length of episode (years)	
	Success cases	Failure cases
Modest policy changes	3.4	4.6
Destabilization	4.3	7.4[a]
Disruption of military adventures	1.2	4.6
Military impairment	5.0	17.5
Other major policy changes	1.0	8.6
Totals	3.3	7.5

a. The period for the failure cases is biased on the low side because three cases are still ongoing.

From the cases we have documented, there is clear evidence, summarized in table 5.5, that the shorter the duration of the sanctions, the greater the likelihood of success. Causation may of course run-the other way: the greater the latent likelihood of success, the shorter the sanctions period necessary to achieve results; conversely, a long sanctions period may betray a difficult objective, and, in any event, the longer sanctions are imposed, the more the target country becomes self-reliant and immune to economic hardship, and the better its chances of finding a friendly power willing to absorb part of the burden. The inverse correlation between success and sanctions period argues against the strategy of "turning the screws" on a target country, that is to say, slowly applying more and more economic pressure over time until the target succumbs. In fact, such an approach affords the target the opportunity to adjust—to find alternative suppliers, to build new alliances, and to mobilize domestic opinion in support of its policies.

Recent experience with US sanctions against Nicaragua, beginning in 1981, illustrates this point. Sanctions thus far applied in a measured and deliberate manner have only unified Nicaragua in common support of the Sandinista government. Domestic opposition to the Sandinistas was suppressed, and Nicaragua has become more resourceful in finding ways around escalating US economic pressure.

V. "IN FOR A PENNY, IN FOR A POUND"

Cases that inflict heavy costs on the target country are generally successful. As shown in table 5.6, the average cost for all success cases was almost 2 percent of GNP; by contrast, failed episodes barely dented the economy of the target country, averaging well under 1 percent of GNP. Both averages reflect the heavy costs imposed in destabilization cases which counterbalance the generally minor impact of sanctions in cases involving modest policy changes.

The seeming perverse result in cases involving disruption of military adventures, where the average costs of failed cases are much higher than for successes, reflects the experience of the early League of Nations sanctions against Yugoslavia and Greece. In these two episodes, the *threat* of sanctions succeeded in forcing the invading armies to withdraw, and therefore no costs were imposed on the target country.

A clear conclusion can be drawn from table 5.6: if sanctions can be imposed in a comprehensive manner, the chances of success improve markedly. Sanctions that bite are sanctions that work. A corollary to this

TABLE 5.6 **Success and costs to the target**

Policy goal	Costs as percentage of GNP	
	Success cases	Failure cases
Modest policy changes	0.6	(0.4)[a]
Destabilization	4.2	1.9[a]
Disruption of military adventures	0.4	1.5
Military impairment	4.3	0.5
Other major policy changes	0.4	0.4
Totals	1.8	0.6[a]

a. In some cases, there is a net gain to the target country, resulting from offsetting trade or aid flows. A large offset in the US v. Ethiopia case accounts for the negative average for modest policy changes, which otherwise would be 0.3 percent. Similarly, offsets in USSR v. Yugoslavia and US v. Nicaragua deflate the destabilization average from 3.3 percent to 1.9 percent. As a result of offsets, the average cost for all failed outcomes drops from 1.0 percent to 0.6 percent of GNP.

conclusion is equally important: sanctions that attract offsetting support from a major power may cost the target country very little and therefore are less likely to succeed.

VI. "IF YOU NEED TO ASK THE PRICE, YOU CAN'T AFFORD THE YACHT."

The more it costs a sender country to impose sanctions, the less likely it is that the sanctions will succeed. This conclusion finds some support in the summary in table 5.7.

TABLE 5.7 **The price of success**

Policy goal	Cost to sender index	
	Success cases	Failure cases
Modest policy changes	1.6	1.6
Destabilization	1.6	1.9
Disruption of military adventures	1.5	2.2
Military impairment	4.0	3.3
Other major policy changes	1.0	2.3
Totals	1.7	2.1

The costs imposed on domestic firms in the sender country are generally higher in cases that fail than those that succeed. The exceptions arise in the case of the two world wars. In most other instances, the cost to the sender country in successful episodes is insignificant, and often the short-term result is a net gain.

The basic conclusion from table 5.7 is clear: a country should shy away from deploying sanctions when the costs to itself are high. Countries that shoot themselves in the foot do not mortally wound their intended targets.

By extension, the results suggest that an analysis should be undertaken by the sender government before invoking sanctions, in order to ensure that sanctions do not impose unduly concentrated costs on particular domestic groups. An obvious example of actions to avoid is the retroactive application of sanctions to cancel existing contracts, which inevitably are painful to individual commercial firms.

Sanctions episodes that are least costly to the sender, and at the same time, most successful, are often those that make use of financial leverage—manipulating aid flows, denying official credits, or, at the extreme, freezing assets—rather than trade controls. Table 5.8, which compares the incidence of success by the type of sanction, bears this out. Financial leverage was deployed in 76 percent of the success cases; by comparison, export and import controls were each employed in only 42 percent of these cases. In destabilization cases, where sender countries were successful 50 percent of the time, financial controls were imposed in every case except one. In failed cases, export controls were the preferred weapon, with import and financial controls also used roughly half the time. Import controls are rarely used in isolation from export controls; accordingly it is difficult to say which form of trade control is more closely associated with successful episodes.

TABLE 5.8   **Success and type of sanction**

	Frequency of use (percentage)		
	Total cases[a]	Success cases	Failure cases
Export controls	60	42	72
Import controls	41	42	40
Financial controls	65	76	58

a. Many cases involve the use of more than one type of sanction.

VII. "MORE IS LESS."

Economic sanctions are often deployed in conjunction with other measures directed against the target: covert action, or quasi-military measures, or regular military operations. As shown in table 5.9, these companion measures are used most frequently in episodes involving destabilization and impairment of military potential. By contrast, companion policies are almost never used in cases involving modest policy changes, and are used in less than half the disruption and major policy change cases. On balance, there is little evidence that covert and military actions, when used in parallel with economic sanctions, tip the scales significantly in favor of success.

TABLE 5.9   **Success and companion policies**

	Incidence of companion policies (percentage)	
Policy goal	Success cases	Failure cases
Modest policy changes	7	0
Destabilization	56	78
Disruption of military adventures	17	56
Military impairment	100	67
Other major policy changes	0	40
Totals	27	40

VIII. "TOO MANY COOKS SPOIL THE BROTH."

The greater the number of countries needed to implement the denial measures, the less likely sanctions will be effective. Contrary to conventional wisdom, multilateral sanctions are not frequently associated with success.

In a sense, the importance of international cooperation is overplayed. Basically, a country looks to its allies for help because its goals are ambitious; in cases involving more modest goals, such cooperation is not needed. These conclusions are borne out in table 5.10. On the average, the degree of international cooperation is somewhat *less* in success cases than in failed cases.

Without significant cooperation from one's allies, the likelihood of success in the two groups involving "high" policy goals is remote. However, international cooperation does not guarantee success even in these cases, as

TABLE 5.10   **Success and international cooperation**

	International cooperation index	
	Success cases	Failure cases
Modest policy changes	1.3	1.5
Destabilization	1.8	2.3
Disruption of military adventures	1.8	2.4
Military impairment	4.0	3.0
Other major policy changes	3.0	1.7
Totals	1.7	2.0

evidenced from the long history of strategic controls against the USSR and COMECON, and the Arab League's futile boycott of Israel.

In successful episodes involving policy goals in the first three categories, the index of international cooperation was generally lower than in failed episodes. In other words, when a sender country thought it necessary to seek and obtain cooperation from other countries, it was probably pursuing a sufficiently difficult objective that the prospects for ultimate success were not bright.

To be sure, international cooperation serves three useful functions: it increases the moral suasion of the sanction; it helps isolate the target country from the global community; and it preempts foreign backlash, thus minimizing corrosive friction within the alliance. These observations suggest that forced international "cooperation" brought about by the heavy hand of extraterritorial controls will seldom yield desirable results. Sanctions should be either deployed unilaterally—because the impact on one's allies is slight; or they should be designed in cooperation with one's allies—in order to reduce backlash and evasion.

IX.   "LOOK BEFORE YOU LEAP."

The sender government should think through its means and objectives *before* taking a final decision to deploy sanctions. The sender country should be confident that what it wants to achieve is within its grasp, that it can impose sufficient economic pain to command the attention of the target country, that its efforts will not simply prompt offsetting policies by other major powers, and that the sanctions will not impose insupportable costs on domestic constituents and foreign allies. A successful sanctions episode will bring the leader of the sender country respect abroad and acclaim at home; a failed episode will tarnish his reputation in all quarters.

"Do's and Don'ts"

Here is our short list of "do's and don'ts" for the architects of sanctions policies:

(1) Don't bite off more than you can chew.

(2) Don't pick on someone your own size.

(3) Do pick on the weak and helpless.

(4) Do impose the maximum cost on your adversary.

(5) Do apply sanctions decisively and with resolution.

(6) Don't pay too high a price for sanctions.

(7) Don't suppose that, where sanctions will fail, companion policies will necessarily succeed.

(8) Don't exaggerate the role of international cooperation: it helps, but when sanctions are likely to succeed you don't need it, and when you do need it, you usually won't get it.

(9) Do plan carefully.

"FOREWARNED IS FOREARMED."

Appendices

Appendix A

$$\boxed{\text{C A S E}}$$

Case 35–1 United Kingdom and League of Nations v. Italy

(1935–36: Ethiopia)

CHRONOLOGY OF KEY EVENTS

5 December 1934	Italian and Ethiopian forces clash at Wal-Wal over disputed border between Abyssinia and Italian Somaliland. (Doxey 46; Zimmern 436)
December 1934– October 1935	France and Britain seek a solution within Ethiopian context using Anglo-French-Italian Treaty of 1906 as a framework. (Doxey 46)
3 January 1935	Ethiopia appeals to League Council under Article 11 concerning Wal-Wal incident; the issues are submitted to arbitration under Italian-Ethiopian treaty of 1928 without results. (Highley 107; Doxey 46)
17 March 1935	Hitler introduces conscription in Germany, violating Treaty of Versailles. (Doxey 47)
September 1935	League appoints Committee of Five (United Kingdom, France, Poland, Spain, Turkey) under Article 15:3 to investigate Ethiopian complaint. Prime Minister Laval (France) insists in private meetings with British that no measures that might lead to war should be taken. This position is known to Italy by 12 October 1935. (Highley 10, 100)
5 October 1935	Italy invades Ethiopia. (Highley 10)
7 October 1935	League of Nations Committee of Six (appointed 5 October 1935) finds Italy guilty of violating Article 12. (Highley 10)

11 October 1935   League approves Proposal Number 1, embargoing supply of arms to Italy. (Renwick 12; Highley 14)

19 October 1935   League approves Proposal Number 2, prohibiting loans and credits to Government of Italy and quasi-public organizations; Proposal Number 3 (effective 18 November 1935), prohibiting imports from Italy; Proposal Number 4 (effective 18 November 1935) embargoing a limited range of exports to Italy, including rubber, certain minerals, transport animals, but *not* including coal, oil, or steel (moreover, extensive exemptions are provided for fulfilling contracts when goods are partly paid for); Proposal Number 5, providing vague mutual assistance measures for countries disrupted by sanctions. (Renwick 12; Highley 78–92)

2 November 1935   League considers Proposal Number 4A, adding coal, oil, pig iron, and steel to embargoed exports; Prime Minister Laval requests and obtains deferral of decision. League approves Proposal Number 4B, obligating members to survey their trade and control abnormal increases in traffic with Italy through third countries. (Renwick 13–14)

7 December 1935   Foreign Secretary Hoare (Britain) and Prime Minister Laval (France) meet secretly in Paris to work out agreement for partial cession of Ethiopia to Italy; proposals are leaked, causing a scandal in the United Kingdom; Hoare resigns on 18 December 1935. (Renwick 16)

12 February 1936   Estimates circulated that oil sanctions would require 12–14 weeks to be effective provided that the US participated; however Hoare-Laval proposal of 7 December 1935 calling for a partial cession of Ethiopia to Italy had undercut the possibility of US participation. (Renwick 16)

2 March 1936   Anthony Eden advocates oil sanctions in the Sanctions Committee; Cabinet colleagues and French block the idea for fear of starting a major European war. (Renwick 17–18)

7 March 1936   Hitler denounces Locarno Treaty; German troops occupy the Rhineland. (Renwick 17)

15 April 1936   League addresses "supreme appeal" to Italy to cease hostilities, but Italian delegation to League insists on *de facto* recognition of military position. (Highley 110, 117)

5 May 1936   Italian troops enter Addis Ababa. (Renwick 17)

4 July 1936   League of Nations discontinues sanctions by a vote of 44–1 (Ethiopia). (Renwick 18)

GOALS OF SENDER COUNTRY

August-October 1935   According to statements in the British cabinet the "psychological effect on Signor Mussolini and the Italian people cannot fail to be very great." (Renwick 12)

Late 1935   "There was strong resistance within the international banking community to more drastic action. Italy's large outstanding foreign debt rendered the creditor countries anxious to avoid precipitating a repudiation." (Renwick 19)

2 December 1935   Cabinet statement of Prime Minister Baldwin concerning the efficacy of oil sanctions: "The object of an oil sanction was to stop the war. If war could be stopped by making the peace, that would be better." (Renwick 16)

29 May 1936   Cabinet statement of British Prime Minister Baldwin: keeping sanctions in force would not likely have any effect on Mussolini "except to make matters worse . . . . The difficulty was one of face-saving and public opinion in this country." (Renwick 17)

26 June 1936   Winston Churchill: "First, the Prime Minister had declared that sanctions meant war; secondly, he was resolved there must be no war; and thirdly, he decided upon sanctions." (Renwick 23)

RESPONSE OF TARGET COUNTRY

2 October 1935   Speech by Mussolini: "At the League of Nations, they dared to speak of sanctions. To sanctions of an economic character we will reply with our discipline, with our sobriety, and with our spirit of sacrifice. To sanctions of a military character we will reply with orders of a military character." However, Mussolini later told Hitler privately that if the League had followed Eden and imposed oil sanctions, Italy would have had to withdraw. (Renwick 18, 108–9)

November 1935   Fascist Grand Council states its "implacable resistance" to sanctions and its determination to "reveal to the world the Roman virtue of the Italian people in the year 14 of the Fascist era." Sir Eric Drummond, British Ambassador to Italy is duly persuaded of Italian intransigence: "In their present mood, Signor Mussolini and the Italian people are capable of committing suicide if this seems the only alternative to climbing down." (Highley 106; Renwick 24)

24 November 1935   Le Temps: "Authoritative opinion has it that the Italian ambassador warned of the danger to Franco-Italian relations which would result from application of Proposal IVA, and that, in consequence, M. Laval suggested to Sir George the postponement of the proposed meeting of the Committee of Eighteen." Proposal 4A, which would have extended sanctions to oil, coal, and steel, was never implemented. (Highley 107)

1935–1936   Summary by Highley of Italian attitude: "Mussolini, confident that war would be avoided by members of the League at any cost and emboldened by M. Laval's voeu that the most severe economic measures be withheld until Italy checked new efforts at conciliation, was enabled to ward off increased sanctions by threats of war or hints of a conciliatory attitude." (Highley 101, 105) According to Walter: "Political and economic measures were instituted (by Italy), including controls over foreign exchange, and an intensive propaganda campaign mounted." (Doxey 107; F. Walter 650–51)

February 1936   Italian delegate to League, Bova-Scoppa, warned M. Flandin, French delegate, that oil sanctions might cause Italy to withdraw from League and denounce the military agreement that was corollary to the Franco-Italian pact of 7 January 1935. (Highley 113)

ATTITUDE OF OTHER COUNTRIES

50 members of League of Nations
Approve sanction measures on 12 October 1935 and 19 October 1935; report progress toward implementation by 31 October 1935. (Renwick 12)

Austria, Hungary, Albania (League members)
> Refuse to apply sanctions for political and security reasons. (Highley 75–76)

Switzerland (League member)
> Refuses to apply Proposal 3 for neutrality reasons, but gives assurances that trade will not exceed 1934 levels. (Highley 75–76, 90)

Ecuador, Paraguay (League members)
> Refuse to put measures in force. (Highley 75–76)

Yugoslavia (League member)
> Applies sanctions and incurs severe trade losses; UK grants partial relief via duty-free entry of poultry and a large bacon quota. (Highley 36)

Argentina, Guatemala, Honduras, Nicaragua, Panama, El Salvador, Uruguay, Venezuela (League members)
> Accept some or all of measures "in principle" only. (Highley 75–76)

Germany (non-League member—Germany gave notice of withdrawal from League in October 1933, effective October 1935)
> Does not support sanctions, but states that it will not increase exports at expense of countries applying sanctions. (Highley 97).

United States (non-League member)
> President Roosevelt's response is constrained by the First Neutrality Act of August 1935. On 5 October 1935, the Roosevelt administration embargoes arms to both belligerents; asks traders not to profiteer and not to trade with Italy in excess of "normal peacetime levels." Nevertheless, United States supplies 6.5 percent of Italian oil imports before embargo and 17 percent by end of 1935. (Highley 95; Renwick 15)

Egypt (non-League member)
> Applies sanctions. (Highley 95)

Brazil, Saudi Arabia, Costa Rica (non-League members)
> Give dilatory responses or refuse to apply sanctions. (Highley 95)

LEGAL NOTES

Legal basis for League of Nations action—Article 16
> "Should any Member of the League resort to war in disregard of its Covenants under Articles XII, XIII, or XV, it shall *ipso facto* be deemed to have committed an act of war against all other Members of the League, which hereby undertake immediately to subject it to the severance of all trade or financial relations, the prohibition of all intercourse between their nationals and the nationals of the Covenant-breaking state, and the prevention of all financial, commercial or personal intercourse between the nationals of the Covenant-breaking state and the nationals of any other state, whether a Member of the League or not."

Legal basis for national action
> In order to implement League measures, 17 states enact special legislation; 29 states act under pre-existing legislation and constitutional provisions. (Highley 66–68)

Bilateral most-favored-nation treaty clauses
> League suggests that bilateral benefits based on initial concessions to Italy (now withdrawn) could also be withdrawn, but that they should be left in place as a matter of mutual support; League also suggests that special favors granted under mutual support provisions need not be extended on an MFN basis. (Highley 62–63)

Commercial rights of Italian nationals
> League pronounces that the commercial rights of Italian nationals are overridden by League action. (Highley 63)

ECONOMIC IMPACT

Observed Economic Statistics

Period	Merchandise exports	Merchandise imports
Presanction November 1934– June 1935	$161.4 million (principal partners) (Renwick 98)	$236.2 million (principal partners) (Renwick 98)
Post-sanction November 1935– June 1936	$105.4 million (principal partners) (Renwick 98)	$163.9 million (principal partners) (Renwick 98)

Miscellaneous

Italy devalues lira by 25 percent in November 1935. (Renwick 19)

Italian net gold sales are $93.8 million in the period November 1935–June 1936. (Renwick 98)

In 1935–36, foreign banks restrict credit to Italy out of prudential concerns. (Renwick 19)

Calculated Economic Impact

	Calculated annual cost to target country
Reduction of merchandise exports by $56 million over six months; welfare loss estimated at 30 percent of face value of trade.	$34 million
Reduction of merchandise imports by $72 million; welfare loss estimated at 30 percent of face value of trade.	43 million
Forced sale of gold reserves of $93.8 million; financial loss estimated at 10 percent of face value.	9 million
Total	$86 million

Relative Magnitudes

Gross indicators of Italian economy	
Italian GNP (1937)	$5 billion
Italian population (1937)	43.4 million
Annual effect of sanctions related to gross indicators	
Percentage of GNP	1.7
Per capita	$2.00
Italian presanction economic relations with UK and France as percentage of total Italian economic relations	
Exports	17
Imports	15
Ratio of United Kingdom and France GNP (1937: $32 billion) to Italian GNP (1937: $5 billion)	6.4

ASSESSMENT

Sir Anton Bertram expressing a pre-Ethiopian view of the League:
> "The economic weapon, conceived not as an instrument of war but as a means of peaceful pressure, is the great discovery and the most precious possession of the League." (Bertram 169)

David Lloyd George on sanctions:
> "They came too late to save Abyssinia, but they are just in the nick of time to save the Government." (Rowland 723)

M. J. Bonn:
> "Stocks on hand, the practice of economies, the development of substitutes, and the purchase of goods with gold, foreign securities, emigrants' remittances and tourists' disbursements kept the country going without too severe a strain." (Bonn 360) "The financial boycott did not imply much more than the moral sanctification of a prudent business-like attitude." (Bonn 354)

Neville Chamberlain, speaking on 10 June 1936:
> Sanctions "failed to prevent war, failed to stop war, failed to save the victims of aggression." Continuance of sanctions was "the very mid-summer of madness." (Renwick 18)

Anthony Eden, speaking to the House of Commons on 18 June 1936:
> "The fact has to be faced that sanctions did not realize the purpose for which they were imposed." (Renwick 18)

BIBLIOGRAPHY

Bertram, Sir Anton. 1932. "The Economic Weapon as a form of Peaceful Pressure." 17 *Transactions of the Grotus Society*.

Bonn, M. J. 1937. "How Sanctions Failed." 15 *Foreign Affairs*.

Brown-John, C., Lloyd. 1975. *Multilateral Sanctions in International Law: A Comparative Analysis*. New York: Praeger.

Doxey, Margaret. 1980. *Economic Sanctions and International Enforcement*. New York: Oxford University Press for the Royal Institute of International Affairs.

Highley, Albert E. July 1938. *The First Sanctions Experiment*. Geneva: Geneva Research Centre.

Renwick, Robin. 1981. *Economic Sanctions*. Harvard Studies in International Affairs No. 45. Cambridge, Mass.: Harvard University Center for International Affairs.

Rowland, Peter. 1975. *David Lloyd George, A Biography*. New York: Macmillan.

Walters, F. P. 1952. *A History of the League of Nations*. London: Oxford University Press.

Zimmern, Alfred. 1936. *The League of Nations and the Rule of Law 1918–1935*. London: Macmillan.

Appendix B

Estimating the Cost of Sanctions: Methodology

This appendix sets forth the basic analytical model we have used to guide our efforts to estimate the costs of sanctions to both target and sender countries. The following discussion focuses solely on the costs imposed on the target country, but parallel analysis also is relevant for the calculation of the welfare costs to the sender country. Our methodology is illustrated by figure B.1.

FIGURE B.1   **Illustration of welfare loss from the imposition of export sanctions.**

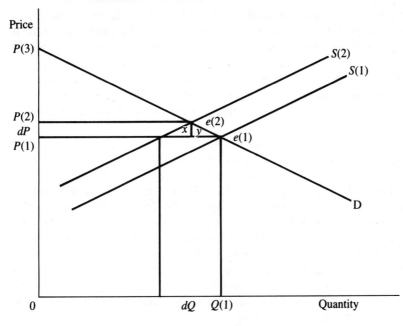

In figure B.1, supply and demand curves are shown for a hypothetical good or service (for example, bank credit) exported from the sender country to the target country. The presanction equilibrium price, $P(1)$, and quantity,

$Q(1)$, are shown by the intersection of the supply and demand schedules at $e(1)$. In the first instance, the sender and its allies deprive the target country of supplies in the amount dQ. Since the sender country and its allies are ordinarily not the only suppliers of the good or service, overall supply availability does not decline by the full amount dQ. Instead, the supply curve facing the target country shifts from $S(1)$ to $S(2)$. The horizontal shift from $S(1)$ to $S(2)$ corresponds to the removal of the amount dQ from the pool of supplies available to the target country. Other suppliers, responding to the abandoned market and potentially higher prices, provide an additional quantity, indicated by x, to the target country. As a result, the net quantity supplied to the target country declines by the amount y. The postsanction equilibrium of price and quantity is $e(2)$; and the postsanction price is $P(2)$, which is higher than the initial price of $P(1)$ by the amount dP.

How much does the target country lose from this sequence of events? In order to answer that question, we must start with a concept used to describe the gains that purchasers enjoy from engaging in market transactions, namely "consumers' surplus." A word on terminology. The concept of consumers' surplus applies with equal force to spare parts, capital goods, and food. It might better be called "purchasers' surplus" than "consumers' surplus." Consumers' surplus is measured by the difference between the total amount actually paid for the quantity consumed (price *times* quantity) and the total amount that consumers would hypothetically be willing to pay if the market could be segregated and each consumer were charged his demand schedule price.

In figure B.1, the level of consumers' surplus before the imposition of sanctions is shown by the triangular area bounded by $P(1)$, $P(3)$, and $e(1)$. When sanctions are imposed, and the supply curve shifts from $S(1)$ to $S(2)$, the trapezoidal area bounded by $P(1)$, $P(2)$, $e(1)$, and $e(2)$ is subtracted from the previous level of consumers' surplus. This loss of consumers' surplus represents the cost that export sanctions impose on the target country. By inspection, it is intuitively obvious that the steeper the slope of the demand curve in the neighborhood of the initial equilibrium price (i.e., the more "essential" the item to the target country and the smaller the range of substitute products), and the steeper the slope of the supply curve (i.e., the smaller the range of available alternatives) the greater will be the deprivation experienced by the target country.

The loss of consumers' surplus is customarily referred to as a "welfare loss." The area of the trapezoid representing lost consumers' surplus approximately equals the rectangle denoted by $Q(1)dP$. Hence, as a first approximation, we may write:

(1) $Q(1)dP$ = welfare loss.

With the use of some algebra, the change in price, dP, can be expressed in terms of the elasticity of supply, Es, and the elasticity of demand, Ed. The elasticity of supply is defined as the ratio between the percentage change in quantity supplied, to a rough approximation denoted as $x/Q(1)$, and the percentage change in price, denoted as $dP/P(1)$. Similarly, the elasticity of demand is defined as the ratio of the percentage change in quantity demanded, denoted as $y/Q(1)$, and the percentage change in price, denoted as $dP/P(1)$. These elasticities can be represented by the following equations:

(2) $[x/Q(1)]/[dP/P(1)] = Es;$

(3) $[y/Q(1)]/[dP/P(1)] = Ed.$

As noted earlier, supply and demand curves that are more steeply sloped in the neighborhood of the initial equilibrium price are characterized by smaller elasticities of supply and demand.

As a further element in our algebraic exercise, we note that:

(4) $x + y = dQ.$

We thus have three equations, (2), (3), and (4), and three unknowns, x, y, and dP. By algebraically solving these three equations it can be shown that:

(5) $dP = [P(1)dQ]/[(Ed + Es)Q(1)].$

Substituting this expression for dP in equation (1), the result follows:

(6) $P(1)dQ/(Ed + Es)$ = welfare loss.

In equation (6), $P(1)dQ$ represents the face value of the reduction in supply from the sender and its allies, before the price paid by the target country rises and other suppliers partly fill the gap.

To summarize, in this simple construct, the welfare loss inflicted on the target country depends on the size of the initial deprivation, the elasticity of supply, and the elasticity of demand. Table B.1 gives some hypothetical values of demand and supply elasticities and the resulting values of the expression $1/(Es + Ed)$. This expression is, in a sense, the "sanctions multiplier," a number applied to the initial deprivation of supplies experienced by the target country in order to calculate the welfare loss.

TABLE B.1.   **Relation between elasticities of supply and demand and the sanctions multiplier**

$(Es + Ed)$	$1/(Es + Ed)$
0.5	2.00
1.0	1.00
2.0	0.50
4.0	0.25
10.0	0.10

By a similar analysis, it can be shown that equation (6) also describes the welfare loss imposed when the sender country closes its markets, and the target country initially loses sales in the amount dQ. In this case, however, the welfare loss represents a reduction in producers' surplus, not consumers' surplus. That is to say, the welfare loss represents a burden on the producers in the target country—a deduction of part of the difference between the market price producers actually receive for the product and the price producers would hypothetically receive if the market could be segregated and each supplier were paid his supply schedule price.

In order to calculate the cost of each sanctions episode to the target country, we first estimate the initial deprivation of markets or supplies, expressed on an annualized basis in current US dollars. We then use our own judgment to estimate the "sanctions multiplier" that should be applied in the context of the particular episode. As a general proposition, we have tried to err on the side of overestimating the appropriate "sanctions multiplier." To illustrate, we apply a multiplier of 1.00 to most reductions in aid, and a multiplier between 0.10 and 0.50 to most reductions in the supply or demand for goods. In a war context, we may apply a multiplier as high as 2.00. The estimates are generous because, in most contexts, the combined supply and demand elasticities would ordinarily exceed 5.0, simply because the target country is likely to be a small factor in world markets. A combined elasticity greater than 5 would correspond to a sanctions multiplier less than 0.2.

General Bibliography

Note: This bibliography lists only general reference works. A detailed bibliography will accompany the abstract of each episode, to be published in Gary Clyde Hufbauer, Jeffrey J. Schott, and Kimberly Ann Elliott, *Economic Sanctions Reconsidered: History and Current Policy* (Washington: Institute for International Economics, forthcoming, 1983).

Abbott, Kenneth W. 1981. "Linking Trade to Political Goals: Foreign Policy Export Controls in the 1970s and 1980s." 65 *Minnesota Law Review.*

Adler-Karlsson, Gunnar. 1968. *Western Economic Warfare 1947–1967: A Case Study in Foreign Economic Policy.* Stockholm: Almqvist & Wikssell.

Ayubi, Shaheen, Richard E. Bissell, Nana Amu-Brafih Korsah, and Laurie A. Lerner. 1982. *Economic Sanctions in U.S. Foreign Policy.* Philadelphia, Pa.: Philadelphia Policy Papers, Foreign Policy Research Institute.

Baer, George W. 1967. *The Coming of the Italo-Ethiopia War.* Cambridge, Mass.: Harvard University Press.

Ball, George W. 1968. *The Discipline of Power: Essentials of a Modern World Structure.* Boston and Toronto: Little, Brown & Co.

Barber, James. 1979. "Economic Sanctions as a Policy Instrument." 55 *International Affairs.*

Bayard, Thomas O., Joseph Pelzman, and Jorge Perez-Lopez. March 1983. "Stakes and Risks in Economic Sanctions." 6 *The World Economy.*

Blechman, Barry M., and Stephen S. Kaplan. 1978. *Force without War: U.S. Armed Forces as a Political Instrument.* Washington: The Brookings Institution.

Brown-John, C. Lloyd. 1975. *Multilateral Sanctions in International Law: A Comparative Analysis.* New York: Praeger.

Doxey, Margaret. 1980. *Economic Sanctions and International Enforcement.* 2d ed. New York: Oxford University Press.

Freedman, Robert Owen. 1970. *Economic Warfare in the Communist Bloc.* New York: Praeger.

Galtung, Johan. April 1967. "On the Effects of International Economic Sanctions: With Examples from the Case of Rhodesia." *World Politics.*

Guichard, Louis. 1930. *The Naval Blockade: 1914–1918.* New York: Appleton.

Highly, Albert E. July 1938. *The First Sanctions Experiment: A Study of League Procedures.* Geneva: Geneva Research Centre.

Hirschman, Albert O. 1945. *National Power and the Structure of Foreign Trade.* Berkeley: University of California Press.

International Institute for Strategic Studies. 1982. *Strategic Survey 1982–83.* London.

Jack, D. T. 1941. *Studies in Economic Warfare.* New York: Chemical Publishing Company.

Knorr, Klaus. 1977. "International Economic Leverage and Its Uses." In Klaus Knorr and Frank Traeger, eds. *Economic Issues and National Security.* Kansas: Regent's Press.

———. 1975. *The Power of Nations: The Political Economy of International Relations.* New York: Basic Books.

Losman, David. 1979. *International Economic Sanctions: The Cases of Cuba, Israel, and Rhodesia*. Albuquerque: University of New Mexico Press.

Moyer, Homer E., Jr., and Linda A. Mabry. 1983. "Export Controls as Instruments of Foreign Policy: The History, Legal Issues, and Policy Lessons of Three Recent Cases." 15 *Law and Policy in International Business*.

Office of Technology Assessment. 1983. *Technology and East-West Trade: An Update*. Washington: US Government Printing Office.

Olson, Richard Stuart. July 1979. "Economic Coercion in World Politics: With a Focus on North-South Relations." 31 *World Politics*.

Marcuss, Stanley, and Eric L. Richard. 1981. "Extraterritorial Jurisdiction in United States Trade Law: the Need for a Consistent Theory." 20 *Columbia Journal of Transnational Law*.

Medlicott, W. N. 1952. *The Economic Blockade*, vols I and II. London: Her Majesty's Stationery Office.

Mitrany, D. 1925. *The Problem of International Sanctions*. London: Oxford University Press.

Renwick, Robin. 1981. *Economic Sanctions*. Harvard Studies in International Affairs No. 45. Cambridge, Mass.: Harvard University Center for International Affairs.

Rosenthal, Douglas E., and William M. Knighton. 1983. *National Laws and International Commerce: The Problem of Extraterritoriality*. Chatham House papers 17. London: Royal Institute of International Affairs, Routledge & Kegan Paul.

Schreiber, Anna P. April 1973. "Economic Coercion as an Instrument of Foreign Policy: U.S. Economic Measures Against Cuba and the Dominican Republic." 25 *World Politics*.

Shultz, George P. Speech delivered 14 October 1978. Reprinted in *Washington Post*, 29 August 1982.

Wallenstein, Peter. 1968. "Characteristics of Economic Sanctions." 5 *Journal of Peace Research*.

Walters, F. P. 1952. *A History of the League of Nations*. London: Oxford University Press.

Weintraub, Sidney, ed. 1982. *Economic Coercion and U.S. Foreign Policy: Implications of Case Studies from the Johnson Administration*. Boulder, Colorado: Westview Press.

Wu, Yuan-Li. 1952. *Economic Warfare*. New York: Prentice Hall.

Other Publications from the Institute

POLICY ANALYSES IN INTERNATIONAL ECONOMIC Series

BOOKS

TEIKYO WESTMAR Univ. LIBRARY

Subsidies in International Trade
Gary Clyde Hufbauer and Joanna Shelton Erb/1984

International Debt: Systemic Risk and Policy Response
William R. Cline/1984

Economic Sanctions Reconsidered: History and Current Policy
Gary Clyde Hufbauer and Jeffrey J. Schott, assisted by Kimberly Ann Elliott/1985

Trade Protection in the United States: 31 Case Studies
Gary Clyde Hufbauer, Diane T. Berliner, and Kimberly Ann Elliott/1986

SPECIAL REPORTS

1 **Promoting World Recovery: A Statement on Global Economic Strategy** *by Twenty-six Economists from Fourteen Countries*/December 1982

2 **Prospects for Adjustments in Argentina, Brazil, and Mexico: Responding to the Debt Crisis**
John Williamson, editor/June 1983

3 **Inflation and Indexation: Argentina, Brazil, and Israel**
John Williamson, editor/March 1985

4 **Global Economic Imbalances**
C. Fred Bergsten, editor/March 1986

5 **African Debt and Financing**
Carol Lancaster and John Williamson, editors/May 1986

FORTHCOMING

Domestic Adjustment and International Trade
Gary Clyde Hufbauer and Howard F. Rosen, editors

Toward Renewed Economic Growth in Latin America
Bela Balassa, Gerardo M. Bueno, Pedro-Pablo Kuczynski, and Mario Henrique Simonsen

Another Multi-Fiber Arrangement?
William R. Cline

The Politics of Anti-Protection
I. M. Destler and John S. Odell

Japan in the World Economy
Bela Balassa and Marcus Noland

International Trade in Automobiles: Liberalization or Further Restraint?
William R. Cline

The Multiple Reserve Currency System
C. Fred Bergsten and John Williamson

Toward Cartelization of World Steel Trade?
William R. Cline

Trade Controls in Three Industries: The Automobile, Steel, and Textile Cases
William R. Cline